PAPH(

TRAVEL GUIDE

2025

Exploring Coastal Delights, Historic Wonders,

and Culinary Secrets: Your Essential Companion

for Every Season

MAP OF PAPHOS

TO VIEW THE MAP, SCAN THE CODE.

4 PAPHOS TRAVEL GUIDE 2025

TABLE OF CONTENTS

9 PAPHOS TRAVEL GUIDE 2025

11 PAPHOS TRAVEL GUIDE 2025

INTRODUCTION TO PAPHOS

I still remember the day I discovered Paphos. It was more than simply another location on a map; it felt like finding a buried gem. Paphos, located on Cyprus' southwest coast, exudes a charm that few other locations can match. From ancient ruins whispering stories of gods and legends to sun-drenched shores beckoning you to stay, Paphos seemed to entice me with each step. When I first visited, I sensed a surprising pull a sense of timelessness that makes Paphos so much more than just a place. It felt like a journey through history and environment, all wrapped in the warm Mediterranean sun.

Wandering the streets of Paphos was like strolling through the pages of a wonderfully drawn history book. Each corner appeared to open up a new tale, from the grandeur of the ancient Tombs of the Kings to the delicate mosaics of the Paphos Archaeological Park.

It was almost as if every stone and column had seen thousands of years and was waiting eagerly to tell its story. I could sense the weight of the history here, yet it was not overwhelming rather, it was compelling and grounded. And, while history hung in the air, Paphos felt immensely alive, filled with both old and new.

The coastline, with its rocky cliffs and golden beaches, seemed like something out of a dream. The sea was a hue of blue that words cannot describe, providing an almost surreal background to my wanderings. Standing at the edge of Petra tou Romiou, also known as Aphrodite's Rock, I realized why legend has it that this is where the goddess was born. There was a strong, almost supernatural aura about it. The waves pounded in a steady beat, and the salty breeze conveyed tales of ancient mythology and everlasting beauty.

Paphos seemed unique not only because of its history and scenery. The people were friendly and inviting, and they appeared truly proud to share their homeland. Their grins, the stories they willingly told, and the delectable flavors of Cypriot food made Paphos feel more than just a destination. It became an experience, one that involved all of my senses and drew me into its embrace.

Exploring Paphos became more than just tourism; it was a trip through layers of culture, myth, and beauty that felt almost surreal. I departed with the impression that I had discovered not only a place but also a sensation that would last long after I had left.

HISTORY MEETS MODERN CHARM

Paphos combines ancient heritage and modern life in a way that captivates all visitors. This coastal town is more than just a destination; it's a vivid tapestry of stories spanning centuries, with each portion of the town displaying unique aspects of its rich history while yet retaining the appeal of a vibrant present. Paphos provides a unique excursion into both history and modern-day Cypriot culture, with spectacular historical sites and vibrant local settings.

There are echoes of antiquity everywhere. Explore the remains of the Paphos Archaeological Park, where ancient mosaics tell stories about gods, heroes, and mythology. These elaborate decorations, preserved for over a thousand years, provide insight into the craftsmanship and beliefs of the people who once lived here. Strolling around these regions is like going back in time, with each stone and relic telling a story of ancient Greek and Roman influence. The Tombs of the Kings are another location where the past is nearly real since these vast tombs were created to commemorate nobility and the affluent in styles that reflect Egyptian, Hellenistic, and Roman traditions.

As you investigate, you will discover that Paphos is not a city fixed in time. Cafés and businesses in the town center are bustling with local activity, combining harmoniously with old buildings. It is fairly uncommon to find modern stores located in structures that have endured for decades. This combination produces an environment in which the ancient and new coexist together. The port district is particularly vibrant, with traditional fishing boats along the shoreline against a backdrop of coastal cafés and inviting walkways. The castle guarding the harbor, a vestige of medieval fortifications, serves as a reminder of the city's tenacity and flexibility throughout history.

Paphos' rich culture extends beyond the historic landmarks. Local markets and artisan businesses demonstrate a strong sense of pride in Cypriot customs. Vendors sell homemade goods such as ceramics, jewelry, and lace, with each piece reflecting a unique tale of expertise passed down through generations. The aromas of local cuisine fill the air, tempting you to sample the island's delicacies, which range from fresh fish to traditional meals seasoned with herbs cultivated in Mediterranean soil. Even the wines here are steeped in history, with farms farming grapes in the same manner for decades.

Paphos is also a place of natural beauty, which adds to its historical appeal. Along with the old remains, there are magnificent beaches and secret coves where you may relax after a day of exploring.

The coastal views, framed by rocky cliffs and boundless blue sea, attest to the island's enduring attraction, a combination of gorgeous landscapes and just the right amount of wilderness.

PAPHOS TRAVEL TIPS FOR FIRST-TIME VISITORS

1. When to visit?

Paphos has a Mediterranean climate, so expect mild, wet winters and scorching, dry summers. March through June or September through November are the ideal times to come because of the lovely weather and reduced crowds. During these months, the weather is mild enough to enjoy the beaches without being too hot for touring. Furthermore, going during these off-peak seasons allows you to see Paphos without the hustle of peak tourist throngs.

2. Currency & Money

Cyprus uses the euro, and ATMs are commonly available in Paphos. Major credit and debit cards are readily accepted in hotels, restaurants, and most shops, but keeping extra cash on hand for smaller establishments and street markets is a good idea. Currency exchange is offered at airports, banks, and currency exchange offices throughout the city. Be mindful of any exchange rates or fees that may apply, particularly if you are using a non-EU card.

3. Transportation Tips

Getting about Paphos is rather simple. Many portions of the city are walkable, particularly near the harbor and historical landmarks. Consider renting a car for longer trips, as it allows you to explore at your own speed. Cyprus uses the British driving system, therefore if you're from a country with right-hand driving, take extra precautions. Taxis and buses are also available, and the public transit system is dependable and reasonably priced, making it simple to go between key attractions and the city center.

4. Accommodation Options

Paphos has a variety of lodgings to suit different budgets. There's something for everyone, from luxurious resorts on the coast to family-friendly hotels and affordable apartments in the city center. Booking in advance, particularly during high tourist season, will assist you secure your desired location and facilities. Numerous hotels and resorts offer stunning views of the Mediterranean and convenient access to nearby beaches, restaurants, and activities.

5. Must Try Local Cuisine

A remarkable blend of Middle Eastern and Mediterranean elements may be found in Cypriot cuisine. When in Paphos, sample native cuisine like souvlaki (grilled meat skewers), halloumi cheese, and moussaka (a layered dish with eggplant and minced beef). Don't pass up the opportunity to experience local meze, a collection of small dishes that allows you to sample a range of flavors in one sitting. For a true experience, dine at traditional tavernas where locals eat and ask for advice on regional delicacies.

6. Main Attractions and Experiences

Paphos is a UNESCO World Heritage site with numerous ancient landmarks to explore. Make sure to explore the Paphos Archaeological Park, where ancient ruins and well-preserved mosaics provide a look into the city's history. Another must-see is the Tombs of the Kings, a necropolis that dates to the fourth century BC. Nature enthusiasts will enjoy the Akamas Peninsula's stunning coastal views, picturesque hiking routes, and isolated beaches.

7. Dress and Cultural Etiquette.

Paphos is a pleasant and tourist-friendly city, however, it is necessary to follow local customs and dress modestly when visiting religious places such as churches or monasteries. Bring a light scarf or shawl because some areas may need you to cover your shoulders or knees. People in Paphos are generally kind and appreciate courteous manners, so a basic Greek greeting, such as "Kalimera" (Good morning) or "Efharisto" (Thank you), can help you interact with the locals.

8. Beach Tips

Paphos is recognized for its stunning beaches, each of which provides a unique experience. Coral Bay is one of the most popular beaches, offering amenities such as sun loungers, umbrellas, and eateries. If you prefer a more peaceful environment, Lara Beach is a more remote region recognized for its natural beauty and as a testing ground for sea turtles. Remember to pack reef-safe sunscreen to safeguard the marine environment, as Cyprus is dedicated to conserving its natural heritage.

9. Safety Tips

Paphos is a secure city for tourists, but you should always take precautions. Be cautious of your belongings in public areas, as petty theft can happen in renowned tourist destinations. If you intend to explore distant locations, such as hiking on the Akamas Peninsula, notify someone about your plans, bring enough water, and wear appropriate footwear. Finally, be mindful of the sun, which may be severe during the summer months; bring sunscreen, stay hydrated, and seek shade when necessary.

10. Language & Communication

While Greek is the official language, English is frequently spoken throughout Paphos, notably in tourist districts, hotels, and restaurants. You'll have no trouble speaking, but learning a few simple Greek words can be enjoyable and appreciated by the locals.

11. Responsible travel.

Respect the local ecosystem and assist in keeping Paphos' attractiveness for future visitors. When exploring natural areas, dispose of waste correctly, minimize littering, and follow established trails. Supporting local businesses, eating at family-owned restaurants, and shopping with artists can all improve your experience and support the community.

ESSENTIAL CYPRUS CULTURE & ETIQUETTE

Since ancient times, Cypriots have been noted for their warmth and friendliness, which makes guests feel very welcome. It's customary to bring a small gift, like flowers or pastries, as a sign of appreciation while you're at someone's house. This small act goes a long way toward acknowledging and respecting regional traditions.

A fundamental aspect of Cypriot society is respect for the family. Many families are close-knit and frequently get together for meals and festivities, particularly in tiny towns like Paphos. When dining out or attending a family get-together, it's customary to thank the host and refrain from bringing up contentious subjects, particularly politics, unless specifically encouraged to do so.

A pleasant handshake and eye contact are the best ways to start a conversation. Although it may be more usual among women, a quick kiss on both cheeks is a typical greeting among friends or close acquaintances. Family, neighborhood gatherings, and food—a significant aspect of Cypriot life—are frequently the topics of casual talk. If you accept an invitation to eat with someone, you will probably be served several short courses, or "meze," which will provide you the opportunity to try a range of regional cuisines all at once.

The religious legacy of Cyprus is a source of pride. It is polite to wear modest clothing when sightseeing, particularly in places of worship like cathedrals or monasteries. Wearing longer clothing and covering shoulders are ways to demonstrate respect in places of religion, even if many locals may not adhere to this rule precisely. Additionally, photography in these locations should be done carefully; it's always better to get permission before taking photos within places of worship.

Paphos's blend of historic ruins and contemporary cafes demonstrates how Cypriot society strikes a balance between traditional beliefs and a modern way of life. Locals will probably be interacting with one another at coffee shops, where they may spend hours exchanging tales while sipping strong coffee. Accept the invitation politely if you are asked to participate because these occasions provide real insight into everyday living.

Gaining insight into the subtleties of Cypriot culture improves your trip to Paphos and enables you to establish a real connection with its residents. Every conversation and shared meal contributes to a culture based on friendliness, deference, and a strong sense of belonging. These small gestures of gratitude and hospitality highlight Paphos' genuine attractiveness and leave visitors with memories that go beyond the city's sights.

CHAPTER 1

Spring (March-May): The Awakening of Nature and Culture

Spring in Paphos is a beautiful season when the region comes to life with blooming flowers and warm temperatures. Average daytime temperatures range from 65°F to 75°F (18°C to 24°C), making it excellent for seeing historical sites and enjoying the outdoors away from the peak summer crowds. The natural scenery is colorful, making it ideal for trekking and sightseeing.

This season also begins with cultural events such as the Anthestiria Flower Festival in May, which is a vibrant celebration of spring and old Greek traditions. The streets are filled with beautiful flower displays, music, and traditional performances, providing tourists with a dynamic experience that is unique to the area. Spring is an excellent season for visitors who enjoy learning about local culture and history.

Summer (June–August): Beach bliss and vibrant events

Summer is the biggest travel season in Paphos, particularly for beachgoers and sunbathers. Temperatures reach an average of 85°F to 95°F (29°C to 35°C) or higher, with bright sky practically every day. The coasts beckon with warm waters ideal for swimming, snorkeling, and other water sports, making this season popular with families and beachgoers.

The summer also provides a variety of exciting events. The Paphos Aphrodite Festival in August is a major draw, bringing visitors from all over the world. This open-air opera event, hosted in front of the renowned Medieval Castle, blends a stunning backdrop with world-class performances to provide an outstanding evening experience. While this season can be hectic, it also provides an opportunity to embrace the city's vibrancy and experience its thriving beachside culture.

Fall (September–November): A Perfect Balance of Warmth and Calm

Autumn in Paphos is popular with tourists searching for a quieter, more relaxed atmosphere. September still enjoys summer's warmth, but by October, temperatures have settled at 70°F to 80°F (21°C to 27°C), providing a pleasant climate for both beach days and sightseeing. The Mediterranean waters stay warm, allowing people to enjoy the beaches through October.

In October, the city hosts the Paphos Wine Festival, a colorful festival that commemorates Cyprus's rich winemaking history. This festival provides a fantastic opportunity to experience local wines and traditional foods while also enjoying folk music and dance. Autumn is an excellent season to visit Paphos because there are fewer tourists and the weather is beautiful.

Winter (December-February): A quiet retreat with mild temperatures.

Winter is Paphos' low season, yet it has a special allure for those looking for a calm retreat. Temperatures range from 55°F to 65°F (13°C to 18°C), which is mild compared to much of Europe, making it ideal for seeing historic monuments such as the Tombs of the Kings or going on scenic beach walks. While swimming is not on the plan, the city's cultural attractions and cafes are open and inviting.

Local activities give warmth to the season around this time. The Paphos Christmas Village and Epiphany events in January showcase local customs, complete with colorful lights, handmade crafts, and seasonal food. Winter offers visitors a quieter, more personal side of Paphos that allows them to interact with the local way of life.

ESSENTIAL PACKING GUIDE FOR EVERY SEASON

Spring: Comfortable Layers and Outdoor Essentials.

Spring in Paphos is refreshing and pleasant, with temperate temperatures that make outdoor exploring enjoyable. Mornings and evenings might still be cool, so layers are essential. Pack lightweight sweaters, long-sleeved shirts, and a multipurpose jacket.

Choose comfy pants and add some shorts or skirts for warmer days. Don't forget to bring comfortable walking shoes, as spring is an ideal season to see archaeological sites such as the Tombs of Kings. Sunglasses, sunscreen, and a reusable water bottle are crucial for staying hydrated and protected from the sun, which becomes brighter as the season continues.

Summer: Light, airy clothing and beach essentials.

Paphos summers can be scorching, so you'll want to stay as cool as possible. Cotton and linen, for example, are lightweight and breathable. Think loose, short-sleeved tops, flowy dresses, and casual shorts. Swimwear is, of course, essential, especially given Paphos' tempting beaches and crystal-clear waters. Bring a beach cover-up, a wide-brimmed hat, and shoes to make it easier to get from the beach to the local cafe. A high-SPF sunscreen and aloe vera lotion will protect your skin from the harsh Mediterranean sun, while a small beach bag will make trips to the beach even more convenient. Consider wearing a light scarf or shawl on cooler evenings by the coast.

Fall: Layered outfits and flexible attire

As temperatures drop significantly in the fall, varied clothing options are ideal. Early autumn can still feel like summer, so lightweight clothing is still appropriate, but later months may require light jackets and sweaters. Consider long-sleeved tops and a combination of lightweight and medium-weight slacks. Comfortable shoes are essential, especially if you're visiting historic sites or doing gorgeous hikes in the surrounding areas. Fall evenings in Paphos can be breezy, so a comfortable sweater or shawl is a must-have. A small umbrella or rain jacket is useful for unexpected showers that may occur as the season develops.

Winter: Warm Layers and Weather-Ready Footwear.

While Paphos rarely sees freezing temperatures, the winters are cooler and rainier. Packing warm layers will keep you comfy. Long-sleeve shirts, sweaters, and a medium-weight jacket are perfect for day travels around town or to the mountains.

A waterproof coat and umbrella will keep you dry during wet days, and closed-toe shoes or boots will keep you comfortable when walking over uneven terrain. Scarves and caps may also be useful, particularly in the evenings when temperatures drop. Winter is a quieter time to visit Paphos, so you'll probably have plenty of space to experience the area's attractions without the crowds.

TRANSPORTATION TIPS: ARRIVING IN PAPHOS AND GETTING AROUND THE CITY

There are multiple ways to get to your lodging or next destination once you land at Paphos International Airport, the main entry point to the city. Taxis are easily accessible right outside the airport and provide a convenient choice, especially for passengers carrying bags.

Depending on the time of day and traffic, the average fee from the airport to the city center is between €25 and €35. A well-known firm, Paphos Taxis provides dependable service to drivers that are acquainted with the main areas of the city. Before embarking on your trip, it's a good idea to check the fare with the driver to prevent any confusion.

The public bus service, run by OSYPA (Paphos Transport Organization), offers a reasonably priced option for tourists on a tight budget. The airport and Kato Paphos, a well-liked neighborhood with lots of sights, lodging options, and dining options, are connected by Bus Route 612. With fares of about €1.50 during the day and €2.50 for routes at night, it's a reasonably priced method to get where you're going. The driver can sell tickets directly to you, but for convenience, have some spare coins on hand. The frequency of the bus service varies, especially on weekends and holidays, so it's best to check the timetable beforehand.

Once you're settled in, Paphos provides a variety of comfortable exploration alternatives. If you intend to see a lot of places, hiring a car could be a wise choice. Due to their wide selection of cars and affordable rates, which typically start at €30 per day depending on the season and the type of car, Sixt and Europcar are well-liked by tourists. You have the freedom to visit off-the-beaten-path locations, such as the picturesque Akamas Peninsula or the secluded beaches surrounding Lara Bay when you rent a car.

Make sure your driver's license is up to date, and if you're not from the EU, find out if you need an international driving permit. It's also a good idea to become acquainted with local driving conventions; driving in Cyprus is done on the left side of the road, which may take some getting used to for people from right-hand driving nations.

To see the city and its environs if you would rather not drive, think about taking one of the local buses. In addition to serving cities, OSYPA buses travel to well-known locations including Coral Bay and the Tombs of the Kings. These local excursions typically cost €1.50, although a day pass that allows unrestricted mobility within Paphos is available for €5. For tourists who intend to visit multiple places in a single day, this is a cost-effective option.

Private hire companies like iTaxi Cyprus provide a compromise between taxis and rental automobiles for a more personalized travel experience. They offer fixed rates and a variety of vehicle options, from regular automobiles to luxury ones, when you book through their app or website. The cost is determined by the route and vehicle type selected, but for longer trips or evening excursions, the pleasure of a luxurious ride and door-to-door service may make the price worthwhile.

Another fun method to get a close-up look at the city's features is via bicycle, especially near the seaside. Paphos Bike Hire has a range of bicycles suitable for both city rides and beach routes, with rentals starting at €10 per day. For active tourists who prefer to explore slowly while soaking in the sights and noises along the way, this option is ideal.

MONEY MATTERS: CURRENCY, TIPPING, AND BUDGETING TIPS

Currency Essentials

Paphos, like the rest of Cyprus, accepts the Euro (€). It is widely accepted everywhere, from large retailers and restaurants to small local businesses and sellers. Before you arrive, consider exchanging some cash to have on hand for modest purchases, particularly at local markets or kiosks. Most hotels, restaurants, and larger stores accept credit and debit cards, so you won't need much cash, but having a few Euros is handy. ATMs are also widely available around the city, and they usually provide decent exchange rates. Be aware that your bank may charge a small fee for foreign transactions, so withdrawing greater amounts at once can save you money.

Tipping practices

Tipping is a customary way to show appreciation for exceptional service, however it is not required in Paphos. In restaurants, a small gratuity usually around 10% of the bill is frequently appreciated, particularly if the service is exceptional. Some restaurants may add a service charge to the bill, so verify before adding a tip. Rounding up to the nearest Euro is normally a courteous gesture for taxi rides, and leaving a modest bit for housekeeping is a pleasant touch at hotels. Keep in mind that locals do not anticipate lavish tips, so a small bit might go a long way.

Smart Budgeting Tips:

Paphos has something for everyone's budget, and with a little planning, you can make the most of your money. Eating at local tavernas, for example, can frequently provide a better and more economical dining experience than more upscale places. If you're traveling on a budget, these restaurants might provide you with a taste of traditional Cypriot flavors without the high pricing. Another advice is to explore marketplaces and businesses distant from the main tourist sites, where costs are typically lower.

Many of Paphos' prominent tourist sites, such as the historic Paphos Archaeological Park and the gorgeous port, are either free or have a low entry price. If you plan on visiting multiple historical places, consider purchasing combination tickets, which can save you money. Furthermore, the city's public transit system is inexpensive and reliable, making it an excellent way to explore the area without having to pay for vehicle rentals or taxis.

Keep an eye out for seasonal discounts on lodgings and activities, as prices might vary significantly depending on the time of year. Visiting during the off-peak season not only allows you to escape crowds but also often results in better pricing on everything from hotels to excursions.

CHAPTER 2

2. NEIGHBORHOODS OF PAPHOS: WHERE TO STAY AND EXPLORE

KATO PAPHOS: HISTORY ON THE COASTLINE

Walking through Kato Paphos, one cannot miss the Paphos Archaeological Park, the city's crown jewel. This UNESCO World Heritage Site covers several acres and houses treasures dating back to the fourth century BC.

The mosaics here are especially stunning; vibrant pictures from Greek mythology, painstakingly constructed with tiny stone tiles, tell stories of love, valor, and divine meetings. Each mosaic is a piece of art, with vibrant colors and detailed designs that reflect the devotion and artistry of its creators. Alongside these mosaics, historic villas once owned by Roman nobility stand as a tribute to the luxury and power of those who ruled these regions.

The Tombs of the Kings are another notable feature of Kato Paphos. Despite its name, this cemetery was not only for royalty but also for high-ranking officials and significant families. The tombs, which are built straight into the soil, are hewn from solid rock and include majestic columns and structures reminiscent of Egyptian architecture. Standing in front of these stone-carved tombs evokes the ancients' veneration for the afterlife, which served as a spiritual link between the living and those who came before them.

The nearby Agia Kyriaki Chrysopolitissa Church adds another dimension of historical intrigue. It was built in the 13th century on the remains of an early Christian basilica, symbolizing the region's spiritual progress. The relics of these early churches mix well with the newer constructions, creating a living chronology.

The Pillar of Saint Paul is located on its grounds and commemorates the location where the apostle was punished for sharing his beliefs. Today, it serves as a humble yet powerful symbol of resilience and faith, attracting visitors from all walks of life who want to reflect on this historical event.

The Paphos Castle, which guards the harbor, is another remarkable feature. Originally erected as a stronghold during the Byzantine period, it has been rebuilt numerous times owing to invasions and natural disasters. The castle's walls tell the story of changing powers, from Byzantine monarchs to Crusaders, Ottoman troops, and finally the British. Ascending its steps, tourists may see the azure waves of the Mediterranean, visualizing the view from centuries ago, when the castle served as both a military station and a lookout.

PANO PAPHOS: LOCAL FLAVORS AND HIDDEN GEMS

The busy tourist destinations along the shore are completely different from Pano Paphos. This upper region of Paphos, which is tucked away on the hillsides, combines ancient attractiveness with a developing sense of local culture. Whitewashed stone homes adorn the streets, with bougainvillea blooms providing sporadic splashes of color. Every store and café in this region gives guests a taste of something special, allowing them to experience the authentic flavors and every day rhythms of Cypriot life.

Discovering Pano Paphos' family-run tavernas and small restaurants, where traditional Cypriot fare is made using recipes passed down through the centuries, is one of the greatest ways to see the city. A trip to a neighborhood taverna here entails trying filling fare like souvla, a kind of traditional barbecue cooked over charcoal for a smokey, genuine flavor, or kleftiko, a slow-roasted lamb.

Every meal is served with freshly made bread and a salad, which is frequently topped with olive oil that is grown nearby. There are plenty of locals who can tell you where to discover the best flavors in town, and dining here is an experience of both flavor and Cypriot warmth.

Wandering around Pano Paphos allows you to find unusual, lesser-known locations that perfectly encapsulate the area. The handmade items that continue to be an integral part of Cypriot culture are displayed in small artisan stores, especially those located down obscure side streets. Locally produced fabrics, elaborate pottery, or woven baskets may be available; these items support the local artisans and provide heartfelt keepsakes. With local galleries and artists' studios where you can view and occasionally buy one-of-a-kind pieces that represent the region's history, scenery, and way of life, Pano Paphos has emerged as something of a creative center for art enthusiasts.

If you enjoy coffee, Pano Paphos has some great coffee shops that serve traditional Cypriot coffee, which is brewed gently over low heat and served in a little cup. The pleasant, community-focused ambiance of these welcoming cafes, which frequently have outside seating, encourages guests to unwind and enjoy the scenery while people congregate there to talk, play board games, or read the newspaper.

Hiking routes that start in Pano Paphos and lead into the surrounding countryside are also a favorite among nature enthusiasts. These trails offer stunning views of the coastline and convey the impression of the surrounding natural beauty of this historic district. Accessible and clearly marked trails offer a chance to explore the terrain that has influenced the history and customs of the area.

Pano Paphos' dedication to conserving its culture is one of its endearing features, as seen by the annual festivals and cultural events. Visitors can see Cypriot music and dance up close at the regular folk dances and traditional music performances. These gatherings, which are frequently hosted in tiny, neighborhood squares, unite the locals, foster a vibrant atmosphere, and let visitors experience local customs.

CHLORAKA: RELAXED BEACHES AND CAFÉS

Chloraka has a unique blend of quiet, beach charm, and local personality that appeals to travelers seeking a relaxing getaway. This beachfront treasure, located just outside of Paphos, is ideal for people looking for a gentler pace, away from the noise and bustle, but close enough to experience everything Paphos offers. The beaches here are known for their laid-back atmosphere, perfect for unwinding with gentle waves and smooth sands. Unlike popular tourist destinations, these beaches offer calm introspection, reading in the sun, or simply enjoying the environment without distractions.

Several quaint cafés dot the coast, each offering a unique interpretation of Chloraka's native charm. These aren't just coffee shops; they're places where you can sit and enjoy a rich cup of local brew, possibly accompanied by a slice of baked pastry or a fresh snack, while watching the calm waves sweep in. Many of these cafés are run by local families, providing a welcoming ambiance and an insight into daily life in the neighborhood. You might even strike up a chat with a local or hear about the best-kept secrets of the area from those who know it best.

Chloraka's environment is naturally relaxing, with a welcoming coastline ideal for individuals who like the simple pleasures of life by the sea. From long walks on the beach to peaceful moments spent staring at the water, it provides a tranquil setting for a relaxing experience. Visitors frequently return to recharge, using the natural rhythms of the waves to set the tone for their days.

Don't miss out on the local delicacies available at the small eateries that line the main streets. Fresh ingredients and traditional Cypriot cuisine are presented with genuine attention and excellence. Whether it's a light fish dish or a filling plate of meze, there's something for everyone to enjoy that captures the essence of Mediterranean cuisine.

Every aspect contributes to Chloraka's welcome atmosphere, where life slows down just enough to enjoy the present moment. This place near Paphos has a charm that appeals to both tourists and locals. It's a spot where you can fully relax and enjoy the subtle beauty and slow pace that make this region of Cyprus so unique.

CORAL BAY AND PEYIA: LUXURIOUS RESORTS AND BEACHFRONT

Travelers looking for a tranquil retreat are drawn to Chloraka's distinctive fusion of peace, beach beauty, and local character. Just outside of Paphos, this beachside gem is the perfect place for anyone seeking a slower pace, away from the hustle and bustle, but still close enough to take advantage of everything Paphos has to offer. With their beautiful sands and soft waves, these beaches are renowned for their relaxed vibes, making them ideal for relaxing. These beaches provide for peaceful reflection, reading in the sun, or just taking in the surroundings without interruptions, in contrast to well-known tourist spots.

The seashore is lined with charming cafés that each give a different take on the local charm of Chloraka. These are more than simply coffee shops; they're spots where you can relax and take in the serene waves while sipping a delicious cup of local beer, perhaps paired with a piece of freshly baked bread or a snack. Numerous local families operate small cafés, which offer a warm atmosphere and a glimpse into community life. You may even start a conversation with a local and learn about the areas' best-kept secrets from the people who know them best.

Chloraka's friendly beach and naturally tranquil surroundings are perfect. It offers a serene environment for an incredibly restful experience, whether you're taking lengthy walks on the beach or just spending some quiet time gazing at the water. Using the waves' organic rhythms to set the tone for their days, visitors regularly come back to rejuvenate.

Don't miss the local specialties served at the little restaurants that line the main streets if you're strolling around the area. Traditional Cypriot food and fresh ingredients are served with sincere care and skill. There is something for everyone that embodies Mediterranean cuisine, whether it's a light fish dish or a hearty plate of meze.

Every element adds to the welcoming environment of Chloraka, where people slow down just enough to savor the here and now. Both locals and visitors find this area close to Paphos to be charming. It's a place to unwind completely and take in the understated beauty and leisurely pace that make this area of Cyprus so special.

CHAPTER 3

3. TOP ATTRACTIONS AND MUST-SEES

PAPHOS ARCHAEOLOGICAL PARK: ROMAN

MOSAICS AND ANCIENT WONDERS

Paphos Archaeological Park is a wonderful window into ancient Cyprus, with Roman mosaics and remains telling stories from centuries past. This park, a UNESCO World Heritage site, is known for its well-preserved mosaic flooring, particularly in the Houses of Dionysus, Theseus, and Aion. Each of these mosaics shows lively mythological stories, demonstrating a blend of history and creativity dating back to the second century AD. Walking through these elaborate displays provides visitors with an understanding of the Roman Empire's cultural and artistic sophistication.

One of the biggest attractions, the House of Dionysus, depicts scenes from Greek mythology in exquisite detail, illustrating the god of wine in festivals that demonstrate the skill and ingenuity of ancient craftsmen. The House of Theseus depicts the Minotaur and hero Theseus in great detail, bringing to life traditions passed down through generations. The House of Aion, which is a little more tucked away, presents additional stunning imagery with its depiction of the god Aion surrounded by important historical characters.

The park contains several ancient monuments, notably the Odeon, an amphitheater that currently hosts plays under the open sky, establishing a dreamlike link between the past and the present. Nearby, the Asklepieion, formerly devoted to the god of healing, and the ruins of early Christian basilicas give further levels of historical discovery, demonstrating how beliefs and architecture evolved through time.

When arranging a visit, it's useful to know the basics: the park is open all year, with different hours depending on the season. From mid-April to mid-September, visitors are welcome from 8:30 AM to 7:30 PM, while during the cooler months (mid-September to mid-April), hours are 8:30 AM to 5:00 PM. The entrance charge is a cheap €4.50, which includes access to all major sites, making it an economical voyage through time. Children under the age of 18 enter for free, making it great for families exploring together.

Visitors are advised to bring sunscreen, hats, and drinks, especially if visiting during the warmer months, as there is little shade throughout the park. Comfortable footwear is crucial due to the rough terrain and the necessity to walk long distances. Early mornings and late afternoons are typically calmer, allowing a more leisurely experience for those who want to explore each location on their own time.

TOMBS OF THE KINGS: A JOURNEY BACK IN TIME

The Tombs of the Kings in Paphos provide an intriguing view into the region's ancient past, evoking a strong feeling of mystery and history. Although these spectacular underground tombs date from the Hellenistic and Roman periods, they are not, as the name implies, royal resting places. Instead, these elaborate burial grounds were designed for high-ranking officials and aristocracy, representing the power and significance of individuals buried here. This huge archeological site is a tribute to ancient architects' creativity, as they excavated tombs right into the bedrock, typically ornamented with Doric columns and spacious chambers that have been remarkably maintained over time.

As you enter the grounds, the first sight of these graves may startle you. Sunlight floods into the open courtyards and chambers, illuminating the once-sacred rooms and highlighting their intricate design. Walking among the tombs, one can almost feel the solemnity with which they were built. The simplicity and majesty of each tomb convey quiet stories of those who were once honored here, whose names have been lost to time but are remembered via the stones that make these ancient structures.

Entry is relatively reasonably priced, making it accessible to both history buffs and families. Tickets normally cost roughly €2.50, which provides admission to one of the region's most important historical sites. The Tombs of the Kings are open seven days a week, with hours varying somewhat depending on the season. From mid-April to mid-September, guests are welcome between 8:30 a.m. and 7:30 p.m., providing plenty of time to explore in the warm Mediterranean light. During the rest of the year, from mid-September to mid-April, hours are extended to 8:30 AM to 5:00 PM, allowing visitors to explore the tombs during cooler times of the day.

When arranging a visit, take comfortable shoes as some spots may be uneven due to the rocky terrain. Bringing water and sunscreen is also advised, particularly during the hotter months. Allow at least an hour to explore the several tombs, each with its unique layout and mood. Photography is permissible, but it's worth taking a few quiet moments to absorb the surroundings without a lens, allowing the history to soak in.

PAPHOS CASTLE AND HARBOR: SUNSETS AND SEAFRONT STROLLS

The Paphos Castle and its surrounding harbor are at the heart of the Paphos coastline, capturing both Cyprus' historical and scenic attractiveness. Originally erected as a Byzantine fort to defend the harbor, this stone building has endured centuries of wars and renovations, each adding layers to its unique past. The vista from its stone walls provides a stunning backdrop for sunsets, with the sun creating bright reflections across the port and sea. It's no surprise that this location is popular with visitors seeking to experience both history and the beauty of the Mediterranean.

As you reach the port, the bustling environment tempts you to slow down, with waterfront cafes and tiny stores lining the route. As twilight approaches, local fisherman pull in their boats, lending authenticity to this crowded seashore. A stroll along the waterfront is best done in the early evening when the cold sea wind and golden hues of sunset create a magnificent setting. For those who want to explore further, the castle is open to the public for a small cost of roughly €2.50, making it an affordable and unforgettable experience. The interior features displays that provide insight into its previous usage, such as its tenure as a prison and its role in regional defense.

The castle is normally open from 8:30 a.m. to 5 p.m. in the winter and until 7:30 p.m. in the summer, but hours may change. An early evening visit gives you time to tour the castle before watching the sunset over the harbor, which is one of the most peaceful and visually appealing portions of the day. Bring a camera to record the panoramic views from the castle top, where the town and beach stretch off into the distance.

THE ROCK OF APHRODITE: MYTHICAL BEAUTY BY THE SEA

The Rock of Aphrodite, also known as Petra tou Romiou, is a timeless landscape with a deep connection to ancient myth. This natural marvel said to be the birthplace of the goddess Aphrodite, is located on the coast between Paphos and Limassol. It was treasured by the ancient Greeks and remains a location where history and beauty are inextricably linked. The legend is that anyone who swims around the rock three times under the moonlight will be blessed with eternal beauty and love. Even if you don't go swimming, the sight will leave you in awe.

The location is open to the public and has no entrance cost. Visitors are drawn here not only for the mythology but also for the spectacular natural surroundings. Waves break against the massive sea stack, serving as a reminder of the stories that have persisted for ages. This site is often most beautiful during sunrise or sunset, when the sky throws warm tones over the water, creating a magical atmosphere.

Consider arriving during off-peak hours to minimize crowds and make your visit more comfortable. Early mornings or late afternoons are great for a more relaxed atmosphere. If you want to take images, these are the greatest times to do it. While the site has no official closing hour, nighttime access may be limited, therefore it is best to check with local resources for information before planning an evening visit.

A neighboring parking lot offers easy access to the viewpoint. From here, a short stroll takes you to the beach, where you may enjoy the views or rest. Swimming near the rock can be difficult due to strong currents, but a dip in the surrounding waters is a wonderful experience just be careful and keep close to shore.

It's a good idea to pack a few basics before your stay. Sun protection is suggested for daytime trips because there is little shade, and appropriate footwear makes the rocky paths easier to navigate. Small cafes in the neighborhood provide refreshments, allowing you to take in the scenery while enjoying a local snack or drink.

AGIOS NEOPHYTOS MONASTERY: SERENITY AND STUNNING VIEWS

Located in the Paphos highlands, Agios Neophytos Monastery offers a tranquil haven rich in natural beauty and history. Founded in the 12th century by the Cypriot hermit and writer Neophytos, this treasured monument is still a functioning monastery, offering a glimpse into the region's spiritual and creative past. Visitors can meander through the tranquil gardens and tour the main chapel, which features beautiful murals that narrate biblical themes and provide insight into Byzantine art traditions.

The "Enkleistra" is one of the monastery's most intriguing areas, a small cave complex hand-carved by Neophytos himself. The tiny, darkly lighted chapel emanates devotion, with faded but captivating murals dating back centuries. Standing here, one can practically feel Neophytos' peaceful reflection, having spent years in solitude within these stone walls.

As you rise to the peak, the views open out to sweeping vistas of the valley below, allowing a peaceful chance to take in the scenery. The monastery's vantage point captures the surrounding mountains and rich flora, resulting in a calm sight that urges visitors to halt and appreciate the island's natural beauty.

The monastery is typically open from 9:00 a.m. to 6:00 p.m. with fewer hours in the winter and more in the summer. Admission costs are reasonable, ranging from €2 to €5 and help to preserve the monastery and its treasures. Arriving early in the morning or late in the afternoon can improve your experience by allowing you to avoid enormous crowds and enjoy the tranquil ambiance.

Public buses travel from Paphos to the adjacent village, and a short cab ride is required to access the monastery. Alternatively, hiring a car allows more flexibility, especially for those who want to see other surrounding attractions. Remember that modest clothes are encouraged as a demonstration of respect for the active monastic community.

ST. PAUL'S PILLAR: A SACRED SITE IN THE HEART OF PAPHOS

St. Paul's Pillar is a powerful symbol of history and faith in the heart of Paphos, beckoning visitors to experience the ambiance of an ancient past that still resonates today. This treasured place is not only a Christian historical relic but also a testament to the long-lasting cultural traditions that have created Paphos.

The tale of St. Paul's Pillar begins with the Apostle Paul's missionary voyage to Cyprus in the first century AD. According to tradition, Paul was tied to a stone pillar and punished for preaching Christianity on the island before converting the Roman ruler, Sergius Paulus, to the faith. This conversion established Cyprus as one of the first Christian territories, and visitors now find themselves transported back in time as they explore this solemn, open-air landmark.

The archeological site housing St. Paul's Pillar is part of the larger complex of Panagia Chrysopolitissa, a splendid Byzantine church erected on the ruins of an older basilica.

It is easily accessible from Paphos' Old Town. The pillar itself is nestled among these ancient remains, surrounded by well-preserved mosaics and remnants of early Christian churches, offering insight into early worship customs and architectural styles. Walking amid these objects, you may have a profound sensation of veneration, as if history is not only remembered but also very much alive.

St. Paul's Pillar is open to the public and free of charge, making it an interesting stop for anybody interested in history, spirituality, or both. While the site is open all year, its hours of operation are generally consistent with daylight hours, which change depending on the season. Visitors should plan to visit in the morning or late afternoon for the most agreeable weather, especially during the warmer months.

Wear suitable walking shoes, as the ground is uneven, with stone walkways and loose gravel in certain spots. Sun protection is crucial given the site's open layout and lack of shelter. Photography is permitted, and many people find the play of light on the mosaics and old stones to be very attractive, so plan your visit when the sun is shining.

Visitors to St. Paul's Pillar will find charming cafés and souvenir shops nearby, perfect for relaxing and pondering after seeing this significant site. The location is easily accessible by foot, bus, or taxi within Paphos, making it an ideal complement to any itinerary. St. Paul's Pillar is not just a historical and religious landmark, but also a calm reminder of the island's spiritual past, providing a thoughtful pause for every visitor as they go through Paphos.

CHAPTER 4

4. OUTDOOR ADVENTURES AND NATURE ESCAPES

THE AKAMAS PENINSULA: HIKING TRAILS AND HIDDEN COVES

The Akamas Peninsula in Paphos provides a unique getaway into Cyprus' natural treasures, with hiking paths and secluded coastline areas that reward those seeking a tranquil connection with nature. The region is known for its natural richness, with winding roads showcasing Cyprus' unique vegetation, wildlife, and pristine vistas. Paths range from simple walks to strenuous hikes, allowing both seasoned adventurers and casual explorers to enjoy the area's natural splendor.

The Aphrodite and Adonis paths are popular routes, each leading to unique panoramas and secluded bays that urge you to pause and enjoy the calm. The Aphrodite Trail, popular among travelers, is around 7.5 kilometers long and offers beautiful views of the coastline, particularly from the high elevations. The walk winds through pine forests, wild bushes, and the occasional orchid before finishing at a cliff edge overlooking the Mediterranean. Alternatively, the Adonis Trail is a somewhat shorter 7-kilometer hike that takes hikers near deep ravines and high cliffs with panoramic views. If you're lucky, you might see rare vegetation and even local fauna, such as the elusive mouflon, a wild sheep indigenous to Cyprus.

Small, hidden beaches at the end of some of these treks offer a peaceful setting for swimming and relaxation. Lara Bay, which is more secluded and accessible only by foot or off-road vehicles, is well-known for its turtle conservation initiative, where visitors may learn about the endangered green and loggerhead turtles that nest in the area. This virgin beach has no services, so visitors must come prepared and leave only footprints to preserve the undisturbed ecosystem.

The peninsula and its trails are normally free to visit, although some guided tours provide in-depth insights into the region's flora, fauna, and history, frequently conducted by locals who give fascinating stories about the area's mythology and culture. Guided hikes range in price from €20 to €50, depending on the length of the excursion and any other services provided. Renting a 4x4 car is recommended for anyone driving into more mountainous locations to visit beaches such as Lara Bay, as regular vehicles may struggle with the terrain. Rental fees for 4x4s vary but often start around €60 per day.

The trails' opening hours are variable because they are outdoor walks with no formal limitations; nonetheless, early morning or late afternoon trips are encouraged for more comfortable temperatures and softer lighting for photographs. If you want to see the sunset over the cliffs, plan a late afternoon hike and leave enough time to return before dark, as the trails can be difficult to travel after sunset.

TROODOS MOUNTAINS: DAY TRIPS TO VINEYARDS AND VILLAGES

The trek through the Troodos Mountains provides a refreshing getaway from Paphos into the region's natural beauty, with exquisite vineyards, tiny villages, and mountain trails. As you travel over the mountain roads, the environment changes from the coastal blues of Paphos to rich green forests, peaceful valleys, and terraced vineyards. This extraordinary change in terrain offers visitors a look into the traditional lifestyle and natural wonders that are only a short drive away.

Exploring the communities spread around the Troodos area, each with its distinct character, provides a true glimpse into local life. Towns such as Omodos and Kakopetria highlight Cyprus' architectural legacy, with stone buildings, tiny lanes, and traditional crafts that appear to be from another century. Local craftsmen frequently encourage visitors to inspect their goods, ranging from handmade lace to pottery, which make excellent souvenirs and provide a meaningful engagement with the region's culture.

The mountain vineyards in this area are a lovely find. Cyprus has a long winemaking tradition, and some of the most well-known Cypriot wines come from these hills. Many wineries here provide tastings and excursions, allowing visitors to try local varietals like Commandaria, a dessert wine with significant historical roots. These tastings frequently involve explanations of old processes and insights into the new approaches that distinguish Cypriot wines. Enjoying a glass in the countryside, surrounded by rolling vineyards, encapsulates the essence of the Troodos region.

Nature lovers can also take advantage of the mountain routes, which range from easy strolls through fragrant pine forests to more difficult excursions that lead to breathtaking views. The famed Caledonia Falls walk is particularly popular, going through shady trees to a gushing waterfall that feels like a hidden gem. Other pathways give panoramic views of the hills and valleys, providing a tranquil setting to appreciate the region's natural beauty.

Troodos' cool mountain air makes it an ideal hideaway during the hot months, while the winters offer a completely different experience. Snow blankets the summits, altering the landscape and even tempting visitors to try skiing, which is unusual for a Mediterranean island.

LARA BEACH: TURTLES, TURQUOISE WATERS, AND TRANQUILITY

Lara Beach, a tranquil seaside sanctuary in Paphos, provides a unique opportunity to see pristine nature alongside gentle waves and vast, clear skies. This quiet shore, noted for its warm, turquoise seas, has a distinct appeal: it acts as a breeding site for sea turtles. Every year, conservation efforts bring these delicate creatures to the sandy stretch, where they lay eggs in protected nests, providing a peaceful delight for tourists anxious to witness natural preservation at work.

Visiting this beach brings a sense of calm, with smooth sand beneath your feet and views that spread endlessly to the horizon. Away from the bigger districts, the ambiance is calmer, attracting visitors wishing to avoid the throng. The adjacent rough landscapes lend a touch of wildness, providing an ideal backdrop for leisurely walks and moments spent observing nature. There are no loud beach vendors or hectic throngs here; instead, simplicity rules.

Swimming in the tranquil waters becomes much more important when you contemplate the conservation area surrounding you, which serves as a reminder of the importance of protecting both the land and its creatures. The beach's slightly remote location preserves it free of huge developments, giving it an ideal area to relax and view the surroundings in its most natural state. Visitors are encouraged to respect defined areas, which provide space for turtle nests and assist in keeping the beach a safe environment for these protected animals.

Reaching Lara Beach is often an experience in itself. Many people choose to explore by renting a vehicle fit for difficult terrain, as the itinerary includes off-road tracks. While the road is not easy, the scenery and sense of discovery make the journey worthwhile. Visitors should take basics because there are limited facilities; the allure of this location is in its natural beauty rather than extra luxuries. Sunscreen, water, and perhaps a nice book are ideal companions for a day spent indulging in nature's basic pleasures.

SCUBA DIVING AND SNORKELING SPOTS

Divers can examine the wreckage of a Swedish ferry that sank in 1980 at the Zenobia Wreck, a well-known location close by. Visitors may see the ship's remnants covered in underwater life, including vibrant corals and darting fish, at one of the best wreck dive sites in the Mediterranean. The Zenobia is best suited for more experienced divers because of its deeper location, and it is advised to go with a certified instructor to guarantee safety.

With the required gear and expert instruction included, tours to this location usually cost between $80 and $150. Dives usually start at 9 a.m. and end by late afternoon.

The Amphorae Caves offer a fascinating exploration option for individuals who enjoy exploring underwater caverns. Divers can swim through naturally formed rock passageways and tunnels in these formations. A short distance from Coral Bay, the caverns also include antique pottery remnants from shipwrecks that are now used as dwellings by a variety of aquatic animals.

Both novice and expert divers can reach the location, however, for safe navigation, it is best to hire a guide. Diving hours are typically from 8 a.m. to 5 p.m., and prices range from $60 to $100, depending on the equipment rental.

Another popular spot is Green Bay, particularly for novice divers and snorkelers. This location, which is well-known for its shallow depth and variety of fish, is perfect for a more laid-back experience. The clean waters allow schools of fish to glide by, making it simple to identify different kinds without going far. Prices for a snorkeling trip here, including equipment, range from about $30 to $50. Visitors can visit the region at any time of day, however, the late morning and early afternoon are the best times to see the pure water.

Because Lara Beach is also a sea turtle protection area, it provides a unique snorkeling experience. As they swim in the shallows, snorkelers may be able to spot these magnificent creatures. Visitors are urged to show consideration for the turtles' environment because of the beach's protection status. In addition to offering a safe snorkeling experience, guides can provide information on the local marine species and environmental conservation initiatives. Sessions are offered from 10 a.m. to 4 p.m., however hours may change based on the weather. A guided snorkel tour typically costs about $40.

Being aware of safety precautions and rules improves the experience. For example, keeping a safe distance from wildlife preserves natural behaviors, and using sunscreen that is suitable for reefs protects fragile marine ecosystems. Because places tend to fill up rapidly during high seasons, it is advised to book tours in advance.

WATER SPORTS: FROM JET-SKIING TO WINDSURFING

Jet-skiing is one of the most popular activities, offering an exhilarating opportunity to explore Paphos' coastline. Rentals are normally available from several beachside providers, with rates ranging between €40 and €50 for a 15-minute session, depending on the season and type of Jet Ski. Operators are normally open from mid-morning to sunset, letting you hit the ocean whenever you're ready. Jet-ski operators will provide safety lessons before you begin, ensuring that even beginners feel at ease on the ride. Some operators provide lengthier sessions with additional direction, ideal for discovering secret coves and more secluded portions of the coastline.

Windsurfing provides a whole different sensation. With continuous breezes along some beaches, Paphos provides ideal conditions for motorcyclists of all skill levels. Beginners can take classes at many locations, where teachers will walk them through the fundamentals of balance and moving the board. A beginner's class normally costs roughly €50 per hour, which includes equipment rental. Windsurfing gear rentals are available for those with experience, with fees starting at around €25 per hour. Several operators provide both morning and afternoon sessions, often extending from 9 a.m. until early evening, allowing you the flexibility to catch the best conditions for your ability level.

Kayaking and paddleboarding are ideal choices for families or groups seeking a more collaborative approach to viewing Paphos from the sea, as they are slower-paced but interesting. The majority of rentals cost between €15 and €20 per hour, with guided group tours often costing between €30 and €50 each. These group alternatives are an excellent opportunity to explore regions that may be inaccessible on foot, such as caverns and calmer beach sections.

Enjoy breathtaking views of the coastline while sailing far above the ocean on this exhilarating excursion. Prices normally range between €40 and €60 per session, depending on the duration of the flight. Sessions normally begin at 10 a.m. and last into the early evening. Some firms also provide images or films of your flight, which can serve as a unique memory of your time in Paphos.

Each water sports activity offers a unique viewpoint of Paphos, from the explosive rush of jet-skiing to the serene flow of paddleboarding down the shore. With alternatives to fit every budget and level of activity, these water-based adventures are a highlight of any trip. Always verify with local operators for the most recent opening hours, prices, and seasonal variations, as these can all vary. Safety is stressed, with high-quality equipment and professionals ready to assist you, assuring a wonderful experience while enjoying Paphos' lovely seas.

CHAPTER 5

5. BEACHES OF PAPHOS: A GUIDE TO SUN AND SEA

CORAL BAY: FAMILY-FRIENDLY PARADISE

Coral Bay's beautiful beach is one of its main draws. Its soft, golden sands and crystal-clear, shallow seas make it an ideal destination for families with children. Parents can relax as their children enjoy the moderate waves and sun-soaked shoreline. To protect everyone, lifeguards are on duty at busy times.

Families can add a touch of adventure by renting paddleboards or snorkeling gear to explore the beautiful marine life just off the beach. These activities are reasonably priced, with rentals ranging from $10 to $20 depending on the equipment and duration.

For visitors wishing to explore Coral Bay beyond the water, adjacent restaurants and cafes provide a variety of local cuisine and snacks, providing an excellent introduction to Cypriot flavors. Several beachside restaurants even provide takeaway choices, allowing tourists to eat directly on the sand. Many of these restaurants are open from morning until late evening, giving users more flexibility in dining times. Expect to pay between $10 and $15 for a dinner, with more luxury alternatives nearby costing $20 or more per person.

As the sun sets, Coral Bay transforms with a touch of magic. The twilight glow over the sea is something that guests will not forget. The neighborhood comes alive with live music at several beachfront venues, creating a peaceful atmosphere ideal for resting after a long day. Although Coral Bay is open at all times, it is best to check the opening and closing times for individual attractions and rentals. Most shops and equipment rentals open around 9:00 a.m. and close at 6:00 p.m., although restaurants and cafes frequently stay up until 10:00 p.m. or later, especially during peak season.

Arrive early to ensure a wonderful experience. Parking is accessible near the beach, however it fills up rapidly during the summer months. Arriving by mid-morning usually secures a good place, and parking costs less than $5 per day. Another option is public transit, with buses running regularly from central Paphos to Coral Bay, making the trip convenient for people without a car.

ALYKES BEACH: PERFECT FOR A LAZY AFTERNOON

Alykes appeals to families, couples, and lone tourists since the waters are clean and tranquil, making it ideal for swimming and paddling. For those hoping for a relaxing day, there are plenty of sunbeds and umbrellas available to rent, with prices ranging from €5 to €7 for a set. While the beach is open to the public, these rentals provide additional comfort, especially during the warmer months when shade is desired.

A selection of adjacent eateries and snack bars are easily accessible along the coast. These establishments cater to a variety of tastes, from light lunches to refreshing beverages, allowing you to experience some local flavor without leaving the beach. Many guests love eating at the beachside pubs, which adds to the laid-back atmosphere and allows them to take in the scenery.

Alykes Beach is open all year and does not charge an entrance fee. The majority of services, including sunbeds, are provided from early morning to sunset, depending on the season. During the warmer months, it is better to arrive earlier in the day to guarantee a seat because it might get crowded. The area's facilities make it ideal for individuals traveling light or wishing to stay an extended length of time without bringing too much gear.

Parking is conveniently provided nearby, but it may be a little walk from the beach. For those who prefer public transportation, various bus routes travel through Paphos and can take you near Alykes Beach, making it accessible without a car. If you want to visit during peak season, you may need to be patient, since the area may be crowded, especially on weekends.

LIGHTHOUSE BEACH: SWIMMING AND SIGHTSEEING

Lighthouse Beach, with its well-kept beach and welcoming tourists of all ages, offers a safe and delightful swimming experience. The water is shallow near the coast, making it perfect for both families and beginners. Lifeguards are on duty during peak hours to ensure safety, while shaded areas and rental umbrellas provide comfortable locations for beachgoers to rest. A charming boardwalk connects the beach to numerous modest cafés, where you can relax with a cold drink or grab a fast lunch while admiring the coastline vista.

Lighthouse Beach is especially popular for its historical significance, as it is only a short walk from the famed Paphos Lighthouse, a landmark with panoramic views of the surrounding coastline. The lighthouse, while not open to the public, provides excellent photo possibilities and is part of the broader Paphos Archaeological Park, which highlights the city's rich past. Exploring these locations provides a sense of discovery as you come across antique mosaics, old Roman structures, and remnants from Cyprus's illustrious history, making it a wonderfully enriching addition to a day spent by the sea.

Lighthouse Beach provides opportunities for more physical sports such as snorkeling and paddleboarding. Equipment rentals are available nearby, and exploring the underwater environment may be a great way to spend an afternoon, with a variety of fish frequently visible along the beach.

Visitor Tips:

Parking is readily available near the beach, however places can fill up quickly, particularly during the summer months. Arriving early can help you get a decent location for your car and on the beach. It's also a good idea to bring water shoes because the shoreline can be a little pebbly in certain places, though the sand is generally soft and inviting. Bringing snacks is encouraged, though neighboring vendors sell light refreshments, ice cream, and drinks.

Open and Closed Hours

Lighthouse Beach is open at all hours, but it is best visited during the day for safety and convenience. During peak season, lifeguards normally work from 9:00 a.m. to 5:00 p.m. to ensure a safe swimming environment.

Pricing

Lighthouse Beach offers free admission, making it an intriguing option for budget-conscious vacationers. Additional fees apply if you want to rent loungers, umbrellas, or water sports equipment. Loungers and umbrellas cost roughly €2.50 each, while snorkeling gear and paddleboard rentals run from €10 to €20, depending on the duration.

CHAPTER 6

6. DELVING INTO LOCAL CULTURE AND HERITAGE

ART GALLERIES AND MUSEUMS: DISCOVERING CYPRIOT ART AND HISTORY

By fusing ancient history with contemporary expressions, Paphos's museums and art galleries provide a strong link to Cyprus's legacy. When you visit these locations, you'll discover both classic relics and modern pieces that showcase the island's many cultural influences, ranging from the Bronze Age to Byzantine, Ottoman, and other periods. The stories told by each exhibit transport you to the customs, lives, and inventiveness of the Cypriot people.

The Paphos Archaeological Museum, which houses an amazing array of items found in and around the region, is one noteworthy location. From the prehistoric to the Roman eras, pottery, jewelry, sculptures, and tools provide insights into daily life. These carefully arranged artifacts exhibit the ingenuity and workmanship of the ancient inhabitants of Cyprus, demonstrating a deft balancing act between usefulness and beauty.

A distinct aspect of the island's artistic legacy is showcased by the Byzantine Museum. This museum provides a glimpse into Cyprus's artistic and spiritual history with its vast collection of holy icons, manuscripts, and murals. The icons' rich symbolism and minute features capture the passion and creative abilities of their makers. Every composition offers an insight into the religious life that shaped Cypriot culture for centuries.

Paphos has a niche for modern art as well, with galleries showcasing the creations of modern Cypriot artists who offer new interpretations of their cultural history. These areas, which display a variety of styles and media, honor the island's artistic diversity. These galleries offer a glimpse into Cyprus's changing art scene, showcasing everything from abstract pieces influenced by the island's scenery to more figurative pieces that delve into cultural and personal identity.

TRADITIONAL MUSIC AND DANCE EVENTS

Folk dances are one of the most intriguing characteristics. Dancers, often clothed in original clothes, perform routines using steps that have been meticulously preserved over the years. Each dance is unique, drawing inspiration from various sections of Cyprus and providing insight into the island's history and culture. Whether it's a quick-footed syrtos or a lively zeibekiko, the dance conveys the spirit of resilience, joy, and connection that this region's inhabitants share. Watching these performances is like seeing a living piece of history.

Local festivals, which are frequently held outdoors, provide some of the best opportunities to see these musical and dance performances. These celebrations greet tourists with open arms and invite them to enjoy the island's hospitality. The Paphos Aphrodite Festival, for example, combines music, dance, and theater against the breathtaking backdrop of the historic castle. Smaller, village-based festivals focus on folk traditions and provide a close-up look at the rituals that continue to shape life in Cyprus today.

For guests, attending one of these events provides more than just amusement. It's an opportunity to engage with people, learn their pride in their heritage, and participate in a spirit of solidarity and joy. The sounds, motions, and colors of these gatherings frequently make an indelible imprint, reminding visitors that some experiences cannot be captured in a photograph and must be felt.

THE WINE VILLAGES OF PAPHOS: A TASTE OF CYPRUS

The wine villages of Paphos, situated over the slopes and valleys of the Troodos Mountains, provide a unique view into Cyprus's centuries-old winemaking traditions. Each hamlet is unique in its attractiveness, with its personality and narrative, and welcomes guests with a warmth that embodies the Cypriot soul. As you travel through these picturesque locations, you'll learn about ancient vines, sample delicious flavors made from indigenous grapes, and immerse yourself in a traditional atmosphere.

Winemaking is more than a trade-in these villages; it is a way of life that has been passed down through centuries. Small, family-run wineries can be found nestled among stone cottages and narrow alleys, where skillful hands have cared for the soil for centuries.

Vines flourish in the mineral-rich soil and bathe in the Mediterranean sun, producing grapes that give Cypriot wines their particular flavor. Two of the best-known types are Xynisteri, a crisp white, and Mavro, a rich, powerful red. Both have qualities that represent the island's distinct terroir and are frequently consumed with local cuisine that complements their flavors.

A normal day in a Paphos wine hamlet takes you near to the winemaking process. Traditional and modern processes merge perfectly as professional vintners describe how grapes are transformed from vine to bottle. Many vineyards have tours that allow you to watch grape crushing, fermentation, and maturing in cool basements. During tastings, locals share their enthusiasm, urging you to sample the strong reds and sparkling whites that reflect the island's unique terrain.

These settlements show a lot about the region's history. Narrow alleyways lead to historic churches, renovated stone buildings, and tiny tavernas serving authentic Cypriot food, with flavors that complement the local wines. These meals frequently include items grown in the neighboring fields, creating a fresh, local flavor that emphasizes the relationship between the land and its produce. These tavernas have a relaxing and welcoming ambiance, which is often enhanced by traditional music, adding to the overall delight.

Wine festivals throughout the year offer a unique opportunity to witness local celebrations firsthand. At these colorful celebrations, winemakers display their current vintages while also providing a taste of regional culture through music, dance, and Cypriot hospitality. These events highlight not only the passion of local winemakers but also the community's tight relationship with its soil.

Visiting Paphos' wine villages provides a sensory trip through the flavors, fragrances, and stories that contribute to Cyprus' remarkable winemaking legacy. The experience is one of discovery, with each glass poured and narrative told revealing a bit more about the island's continuing beauty and character. Whether you're a wine lover or just inquisitive, the wine villages allow you to interact with the land, the people, and the rich history of Cypriot winemaking.

POTTERY, LACE, AND CRAFTS: PAPHOS ARTISANS AT WORK

The effort of local artisans is evident in each handcrafted piece, which captures the essence of the region's tradition. While strolling around workshops, you'll come across excellent potters, delicate lace-makers, and traditional craft artists who use time-honored processes to create each piece. Pottery is particularly important in Paphos, where artisans shape clay into exquisite forms inspired by Cypriot culture. From elaborate vases to beautifully textured crockery, each piece depicts a past influenced by the island's natural surroundings. Cypriot pottery's natural tones and textures reflect Paphos' surroundings, merging perfectly into both contemporary and rustic environments.

Lace-making, another popular art form in the area, enables you to observe the care and precision required. The village of Lefkara, located near Paphos, is well-known for its lacework, with each piece expressing a tale through intricate designs. These linens, whether beautiful table runners or delicate doilies are painstakingly crafted by local artists who have learned the trade from generations before them. Owning a piece of Paphos lace means preserving a bit of Cyprus' cultural character, and these masterpieces are excellent keepsakes that reflect the island's ethos.

Paphos is home to a variety of other traditional crafts. Hand-carved wood items, silver jewelry, and woven baskets are created with commitment and skill, employing techniques that artists have perfected over time. Each item represents a piece of the island's history and exemplifies the meticulous craftsmanship that distinguishes these unique pieces.

CHAPTER 7

7. PAPHOS FOR FAMILIES: FUN FOR ALL AGES

FAMILY-FRIENDLY BEACHES AND ACTIVITIES

1. Coral Bay: A Favorite Spot for Families

Coral Bay is one of the most well-known beaches for families visiting Paphos. Its soft sands and gentle waves make it an excellent choice for children to play safely by the shore. The beach has a range of amenities, including sunbeds and umbrellas for rental, restrooms, and lifeguards on duty, providing families with a safe and comfortable experience. Families can also enjoy a variety of water sports, like paddle boats, which cost around €10–€15 per hour or opt for jet ski rentals for those looking for a bit more excitement, with prices averaging €50 for a half-hour session.

Opening Hours: Coral Bay is open to visitors all day, but lifeguard services typically run from 10:00 am to 6:00 pm during the summer months, ensuring extra safety for families during peak hours.

Tips: Arrive early to secure a good spot on the beach, especially during the high season. If you're planning to enjoy water sports, inquire at the rental stations for any available discounts for families or groups.

2. Latchi Beach: Perfect for a Day of Exploring

Latchi Beach combines relaxation with opportunities for a little adventure. Families can unwind by the sea and take advantage of the shallow waters, ideal for young children. For those interested in activities, there are boat tours available that provide a chance to explore the nearby Blue Lagoon, where everyone can snorkel or swim in crystal-clear waters. Boat tours typically cost around €25–€35 per adult and €15–€20 per child, making it an affordable outing for the entire family.

Opening Hours: The beach is accessible at all times, while boat tours generally start from 9:00 am and continue until sunset. It's best to book these tours in advance, especially during the holiday season.

Tips: Pack some snacks or a picnic, as there are a few scenic spots near Latchi Beach where families can enjoy a meal with a view. For younger children or less experienced swimmers, life jackets are available on the boats, ensuring a safe experience for everyone.

3. Paphos Waterpark: A Day of Aquatic Fun

Paphos Aphrodite Waterpark is a must-visit for families looking for a day full of excitement and entertainment. This waterpark features a wide range of attractions, including lazy rivers, wave pools, and designated splash zones for young children. With slides of all sizes, children and adults alike can enjoy hours of fun in the water. Adult tickets cost about €30, children ages 3 to 12 €20, and children under three enter free of charge. Various family packages are also available, providing value for larger groups.

Opening Hours: The waterpark operates from 10:00 am to 5:30 pm daily, with extended hours until 6:00 pm during peak summer months.

Tips: To make the most of your day, plan to arrive early when the park is less crowded. Bringing waterproof sunscreen is essential, as the Cypriot sun can be strong, especially during midday. Lockers are available for a small fee, so you can keep your belongings safe while enjoying the attractions.

4. Alykes Beach: Relaxing by the Sea with Nearby Amenities

Alykes Beach is another family-friendly destination, known for its convenient location close to various cafés and restaurants. The calm, shallow waters are ideal for young children, and the beach's proximity to amenities makes it easy to take breaks for meals or refreshments. Families can rent sunbeds and umbrellas for around €7 per set, making it an affordable spot to relax by the sea.

Opening Hours: This beach is open all day, and most nearby businesses operate from around 9:00 am to late evening, offering plenty of options for dining and refreshments.

Tips: Consider visiting during the early morning or later in the afternoon for a quieter experience, as the beach can become busy during peak hours. Nearby shops offer inflatables and beach toys, which can be a great way to keep younger children entertained.

5. Kato Paphos Playground and Picnic Area

The Kato Paphos area features a well-maintained playground and picnic area, where children can enjoy various play structures and open spaces to run around. This area is perfect for families who want to relax while children burn off some energy in a safe environment. Entry to the playground is free, and it's conveniently located near the harbor, allowing families to explore nearby attractions afterward.

Opening Hours: The playground is open from 9:00 am to sunset, making it an ideal spot for morning or late afternoon outings.

Tips: Bring along some snacks or a picnic, as there are tables available for families to use. Sunscreen and hats are recommended, as shaded areas can be limited.

KID-FRIENDLY HISTORICAL SITES AND PARKS

Paphos Archaeological Park

This vast park introduces young visitors to the wonders of ancient cultures through mosaics, temples, and ruins. Kids can explore the historical remains while parents can share stories of ancient times. Entry fees are reasonable, with free entry for children under a certain age, making it an affordable family destination.

Visiting hours typically begin around 8:30 a.m., and the park stays open until the late afternoon, but it's best to check the current schedule as it may change with the seasons. Comfortable footwear and sun protection are recommended, as the park is expansive and largely outdoors.

Aphrodite's Rock and Beach

This iconic coastal site holds an interesting mythological tale and makes for a memorable stop with kids. Legend has it that the goddess Aphrodite was born from the sea foam at this very spot.

The area is free to visit, though parking close may have a small fee. Mornings and late afternoons are ideal times to escape midday crowds, and the beach area offers a chance to cool off by the water. Children especially enjoy discovering the rock formations and shallow waters along the beach. Pack a picnic or snacks, as the area has limited services.

Tombs of the Kings

Although the name might sound eerie, the Tombs of the Kings is a captivating place for children to walk and imagine life in ancient times. It's an intriguing labyrinth of tombs carved into the rock, giving children a glimpse of ancient architecture and burial customs. Admission is budget-friendly, and children can usually join for free or at a reduced rate. The site opens around 8:30 a.m., and it's advised to come early for cooler temperatures and fewer crowds. Since the site can be uneven, having sturdy shoes is important. Families can combine this visit with a trip to nearby beaches or restaurants for a well-rounded day out.

Eleouthkia Park

This park combines aspects of Cyprus's natural flora with entertaining activities for young ones. Families can wander through beautifully landscaped grounds that feature local plants, and there's also a mini-zoo, play areas, and participatory workshops on traditional crafts. Entrance fees are modest, with discounts for children, and the park is open from morning until early evening, with hours changing slightly by season.

It's an ideal spot for a leisurely family day surrounded by nature. Bringing drinks, snacks, and sunscreen will ensure everyone stays comfortable, especially during warmer months.

Paphos Zoo

Paphos Zoo, while a bit outside the city center, is a great choice for a day trip. With its variety of animals and interactive feedings, children will love watching creatures from around the world in a family-friendly setting. Ticket prices vary, with discounts offered for children and families.

The zoo opens mid-morning and stays open until evening, giving ample time to explore without rushing. Be sure to check the daily schedules for animal feedings, as they offer chances for children to get closer to some of the animals. Hats and water are suggested, as many enclosures are outdoors.

Municipal Gardens and Playground

Located within the city, this place offers a welcome break from structured sightseeing. The playground, shaded areas, and grassy lawns provide a place for children to run and play freely. Nearby bars allow parents to relax while keeping an eye on the kids. The gardens are free to join and open from early morning until late in the evening, making it a flexible choice for families. It's an ideal spot to unwind, especially for families who want a relaxing day without organized activities.

Byzantine Museum

While museums may not be every child's first choice, the Byzantine Museum in Paphos offers a quiet and interesting experience with its displays of ancient icons, frescoes, and artifacts. It's a smaller museum, making it doable for families with young children. Admission fees are affordable, and the museum usually opens mid-morning until early afternoon. Visiting on a cooler day or early in the morning is suggested, as there's plenty to see without feeling rushed.

ANIMAL ENCOUNTERS AND PETTING FARMS

Animal farms are carefully designed to allow for direct interaction, allowing guests to spend time with the animals and learn about their histories and behaviors. From goats and bunnies to more exotic inhabitants like llamas and alpacas, these locations frequently have amiable, approachable creatures who love interacting with people. The experience is made more instructive by the presence of informed staff members who are available to explain their expertise in each species while guests engage with the animals.

These interactions are especially engaging for younger guests. Under close supervision, kids can safely engage with gentle animals, strengthening their bond with the natural world.

Kids can give animals little gifts at feeding times, which are typically planned throughout the day, and watch how the animals react to careful care. Some places could have pony or donkey rides, which provide a straightforward but thrilling addition to the day.

These petting farms frequently serve as educational and conservation hubs. Many seek to increase visitors' understanding of animal care and foster a deeper respect for the environment and the creatures that rely on it. For tourists looking for a more in-depth knowledge of wildlife and its significance in a practical, engaging environment, it's a rewarding encounter.

Some places in the Paphos area provide greater animal encounters with more exotic species in addition to petting farms. You might be able to observe raptors, big cats, or even elephants at zoos and wildlife parks. Visitors can depart with a deeper comprehension of the natural world thanks to planned presentations, feeding demonstrations, and educational talks.

Minigolf in Paphos

Mini golf is a great way for both youngsters and adults to spend a few hours working on their putting skills. Paphos features various well-designed courses with unique obstacles, colorful scenery, and diverse themes that add a creative edge. You can choose from conventional greens to pirate-inspired excursions where the challenge is navigating challenging obstacles.

Prices normally range from €5 to €10 per person, making it an affordable and entertaining visit. These courses typically open in the middle of the day, around 10:00 a.m., and close at 8:00 or 9:00 p.m., though hours might vary seasonally, so check beforehand.

Tips for a memorable mini golf experience:

Go early in the morning or late in the afternoon for quieter hours, and bring sunblock and water because some courses offer minimal shade. These venues also offer a relaxing, casual atmosphere, ideal for friendly competitions or unwinding after a long day.

Water Parks in Paphos

Water parks in Paphos take the excitement to the next level, featuring activities for all ages. Expect a variety of exhilarating water slides, soothing meandering rivers, and splash sections ideal for children. Paphos Aphrodite Waterpark, one of the primary attractions, is a popular choice among visitors because of its vast selection of rides, wave pools, and activity spaces.

The park's entry rates range from €30 to €40 for adults and slightly less for children, with family passes available to help decrease costs. The park is open from May to October, from 10:00 AM to 6:00 PM, though these hours may be extended during high summer months.

Arrive early to obtain shaded seating for a pleasant water park experience, especially if you're going during the high summer months. Many visitors find it advantageous to hire lockers to keep their belongings secure and tubes to avoid long queues at particular attractions. Bringing water-friendly shoes is also beneficial for moving around, as surfaces might become warm in the sun.

Adventure Parks and Fun Centres

Aside from mini golf and water parks, Paphos has interesting adventure parks and entertainment centers that will add variation to any schedule. These frequently include a variety of activities such as bumper boats, climbing walls, and arcade games, making them ideal for spending a few additional hours. Prices and hours vary by location, and some adventure parks provide package deals that incorporate various activities for a single fee.

These locations are ideal for entertaining everyone, especially if you have children with you. Look for evening hours throughout the summer when the parks stay open longer and lend a touch of magic to the night with lights and music.

CHAPTER 8

8. FOOD & DRINK IN PAPHOS

MUST-TRY LOCAL DISHES: A TASTE TOUR OF CYPRIOT CUISINE

Starting with Meze, a collection of small meals, you'll be introduced to a range of local delicacies. From freshly grilled meats to colorful dips, meze is meant to be shared, with each dish revealing something different. Expect foods such as grilled halloumi cheese, which is known for its firm structure and savory flavor, as well as tzatziki, a cold yogurt-based dip with cucumber and garlic that goes great with freshly baked bread.

A trip to Cyprus would not be complete without trying Souvlaki. Small chunks of tender meat are marinated, skewered, and grilled, then served with pita and fresh garnishes. The flavoring, a combination of herbs and lemon, offers the ideal balance of savory and refreshing undertones, resulting in a tasty yet simple supper that reflects the essence of island living.

Kleftiko is a must-see for those looking for a more active adventure. This lamb meal is slow-cooked to perfection, with the meat marinated in garlic, lemon, and spices before being wrapped in foil to keep all of the rich juices. As a result, the lamb is soft, delicious, and virtually melts in your mouth true island comfort food.

Moussaka is another notable meal, consisting of layered eggplant, potatoes, ground beef, and creamy béchamel sauce cooked until golden. While some may compare moussaka to lasagna, it has a distinct Mediterranean flavor, which is complemented by the indigenous spices and ingredients that are unique to Cyprus.

Octopus, cooked to perfection, is commonly served with a sprinkling of olive oil and lemon. The tiny burn on the surface highlights the octopus' natural sweetness, and the dish's simplicity allows the seafood to shine. It's an excellent choice for anyone wanting to experience Cyprus's seaside influences.

Vegetarians will enjoy Fasolada, a Spanish bean soup, which is warm and substantial. It's made with white beans, tomatoes, and a variety of vegetables and seasoned with olive oil and herbs, resulting in a tasty, healthy dish that's both familiar and uniquely Cypriot.

Loukoumades, Cyprus' version of doughnuts, are small fried dough balls drizzled with honey and occasionally topped with nuts. This dessert is a pleasant way to end a meal, delivering a taste of local sweetness in a simple but delicious style.

BEST RESTAURANTS FOR TRADITIONAL AND MODERN FLAVORS

1. 7 St. George's Tavern Known for its meze, 7 St. George's delivers a true taste of Cyprus with fresh, locally sourced ingredients. This family-run spot doesn't rely on a fixed menu; instead, plates are crafted daily based on the best produce available, from garden herbs to locally raised meats. Prices range around €20-€30 per person for a generous meal. Open daily from 12 PM to 11 PM, it's ideal for a relaxed lunch or hearty dinner. Because it fills up

rapidly, especially on weekends, early attendance is encouraged.

2. Ficardo Restaurant Blending Mediterranean and international dishes, Ficardo offers a sophisticated yet comfortable dining experience. From grilled seafood to traditional Cypriot salads, the diverse menu is a feast for varied tastes. Expect to spend about €25-€40 per person. The business is open every day from 5 to 11 p.m. Reservation is recommended, especially during peak tourist seasons, as its popularity draws a lively crowd.

3. Laona Restaurant Laona embodies the essence of traditional Cypriot home cooking with a welcoming, warm ambiance. Dishes like moussaka and stuffed vegetables are prepared with recipes passed down through generations. Prices are very reasonable, averaging €15-€20 per person. It's open Monday to Friday, from 12 PM to 3 PM. Arriving early is suggested to avoid the lunch rush and experience the freshest plates.

4. The Lodge Steak & Seafood Co. This unique spot merges steakhouse flavors with Cypriot hospitality,

making it a go-to for high-quality meats and fresh seafood. The menu includes a range of options from tender steaks to ocean-fresh catches, with pricing between €30-€50 per person. Open from 6 PM to 11 PM every day except Sunday, it's a great choice for a special evening out. Reservations are essential, particularly for Friday and Saturday nights.

5. Mandra Tavern This family-owned establishment has been a Paphos staple for over four decades. The menu covers a mix of local meats, seasonal vegetables, and classic Cypriot dishes such as stifado (beef stew) and souvlaki. Meals range from €15-€25 per person, providing hearty portions. Operating from 5 PM to 11 PM, it's the perfect spot for an authentic Cypriot dinner. For an enhanced experience, ask about the daily specials often featuring locally sourced ingredients.

6. Gabor French Restaurant For a fusion of Cypriot charm and French elegance, Gabor is a must-visit. It offers French classics with a Mediterranean touch, including duck confit and escargot, alongside seafood favorites.

Meals generally cost €30-€45 per person. It's open Tuesday to Sunday from 6 PM to 10 PM. Booking in advance is highly encouraged as the intimate setting fills up quickly, particularly on weekends.

7. Sienna Restaurant Known for its fusion of Mediterranean and Cypriot cuisine, Sienna provides a relaxed but refined dining setting. Dishes like lamb kleftiko and grilled octopus highlight fresh, local flavors with contemporary appeal. Prices are moderate, between €20-€35 per person. Sienna is open from 5:30 PM to 11 PM, and reservations are suggested, especially if you're looking for a table with a sunset view.

TAVERNA CULTURE: EATING LIKE A LOCAL

Tavernas in Paphos are the core of Cypriot dining, serving more than just food. These local establishments, which are generally family-owned, offer an authentic experience in which each meal feels like a celebration. Meals at a taverna are about savoring food and connecting with long-held local traditions.

Tavernas provide an open door to history, heritage, and the warmth of Cypriot hospitality for those who want to learn more about Cyprus than the typical tourist destinations.

Dining in a taverna is like entering a friendly atmosphere where time slows down, enabling each dish to be enjoyed. The menu often includes traditional meals made with fresh, local ingredients, with each plate rich in history and flavor. Souvlaki grilled meats on skewers will be paired with tangy tzatziki, a delicious blend of yogurt, cucumber, and garlic. Another popular dish is kleftiko, a soft lamb dish slow-cooked with aromatic herbs until it melts off the bone. These meals introduce diners to Cyprus through cuisine that celebrates the island's agricultural past and Mediterranean traditions.

Meals at a taverna are frequently arranged around meze, a dining style that emphasizes sampling a variety of small plates shared with friends and family. This communal approach to dining promotes connection, and the variety guarantees that everyone has something to enjoy. Meze might be everything from fresh village salads and crispy halloumi cheese to marinated olives and substantial stews. With each meal, visitors can appreciate the effort that goes into preparing food that is both enjoyable and full of local flavor.

Wine is an important element of the taverna experience, frequently acquired from neighboring vineyards that have thrived in Cyprus's peculiar climate for decades. Local wines, such as the sweet Commandaria or a strong red, typically complement the dinner, balancing the rich flavors on the table. Taverns take pride in selling wines that reflect the island's terroir, making each glass an integral part of the experience alongside the meal.

The atmosphere of a taverna contributes to its appeal. Simple decor, pleasant lighting, and, in many cases, a cozy courtyard make it comfortable to relax and eat for hours. On certain evenings, certain tavernas have live music, with traditional tunes filling the air and customers attracted to spontaneous dancing a reflection of Cypriot culture's cheerful, sociable side.

WINE AND SPIRIT TASTING: CYPRIOT WINERIES AND VINEYARDS

With some vineyards growing native grape varietals that are exclusive to the island, such as Maratheftiko and Xynisteri, Cypriot wines have a rich history. Travelers can enjoy the rich, fruity reds, crisp whites, and even uncommon dessert wines at these wineries.

Each wine has a unique flavor that reflects the soil and climate of the area. Numerous wineries have guided tours that take visitors through their wine cellars, where the wines are aged in oak barrels, giving each bottle a variety of levels of complexity. Experienced hosts offer a personal touch by sharing the histories of their wineries, many of which are family-run.

A visit may also involve sampling spirits like zivania, a typical Cypriot beverage derived from grape pomace that has a strong, distinct flavor. Local specialties, such as soft, herbed cheeses or freshly baked bread, are frequently served with tastings to enhance the flavors and give guests a taste of the cuisine.

Joining organized tasting excursions, which take visitors to several wineries in a single day and give them a taste of the island's diverse terroirs, is an option for people who want to learn more about Paphos's wine legacy. Visitors can also experience wines made with care for the environment thanks to some of these vineyards' commitment to organic and sustainable practices.

STREET FOOD, BAKERIES, AND CAFÉS

1. Gyros Corner Paphos

Location: 21 Agapinoros Street

A favorite for quick bites, Gyros Corner serves up flavorful, generously filled gyros. Each gyro costs around €6, making it a budget-friendly option for those seeking an authentic Greek taste in Paphos. Open from 11:00 AM to 11:00 PM, it's ideal for a satisfying meal any time of day. Insider tip: Try adding extra tzatziki for an authentic touch.

2. Zorba's Bakery

Location: 43 Neophytou Nikolaidi Avenue

With an inviting selection of freshly baked goods, Zorba's has long been a local favorite. Specialties include Cyprus sesame-covered koulouri bread, priced at €1.50 each. This bakery is a great place to stop for breakfast or a snack in the afternoon from 7:00 AM to 9:00 PM. Try the olive bread if you're after a local twist.

3. Omikron Brunch Café

Location: 6 Tombs on the Kings Avenue

Known for its vibrant brunch offerings, Omikron has everything from sweet pastries to savory sandwiches. Meals generally cost between €8 and €15. Operating from 8:00 AM to 4:00 PM, Omikron's relaxed atmosphere makes it a refreshing break in your day. The avocado toast, with a unique local touch, is worth a try.

4. Alea Café-Lounge Bar

Location: Poseidonos Avenue

Perfectly positioned by the seafront, Alea offers light snacks and refreshing drinks with a stunning view of the Mediterranean. Prices range from €5 to €12. Open from 9:00 AM until late at night, Alea provides a scenic spot for a casual lunch or a relaxing evening drink. Their Cypriot iced coffee makes for a refreshing pick-me-up.

5. Piatsa Gourounaki

Location: 25 Agapinoros Street

Specializing in street food-style souvlaki, Piatsa Gourounaki is known for its affordable yet delicious offerings. With meals costing around €10, it's a great choice for sampling Cypriot flavors on a budget. Open from 12:00 PM to 11:00 PM, this spot brings a friendly vibe and generous portions. Consider ordering the pork souvlaki for a classic experience.

6. Chalkies Bar

Location: Tombs of the Kings Road

A casual hangout, Chalkies Bar features a wide variety of snacks and light meals, from sandwiches to salads, usually priced between €5 and €10. Its hours, 11:00 AM to midnight, make it a great choice for both lunch and late-night bites. For a refreshing option, try their freshly prepared salads.

7. The Windmill Restaurant

Location: Minoos Street

Serving local favorites, The Windmill is known for Cypriot pastries and simple desserts. Prices for sweet treats typically range from €2 to €5. Operating from 10:00 AM to 10:00 PM, it's an ideal stop for a light afternoon snack. The honey-drizzled loukoumades (Greek doughnuts) are a local specialty.

8. Kafeneio Elladion

Location: Makarios Avenue

A rustic café with traditional Cypriot snacks and light bites, Kafeneio Elladion offers treats like halloumi pita for around €4.50. Open from 9:00 AM to 8:00 PM, the spot offers an authentic taste of Cyprus, perfect for a leisurely afternoon snack. The halloumi pita is highly recommended for its rich, savory flavor.

9. Balkanika

Location: Kato Paphos

This hidden gem is a fusion café that blends Cypriot and Balkan flavors, making it a unique stop for adventurous eaters. Dishes are reasonably priced at around €10. Open from 10:00 AM to 11:00 PM, it's a delightful spot for lunch or dinner. The baked cheese dishes have become a local favorite.

10. Costa's Coffee House

Location: Poseidonos Avenue

Offering a mix of international and local flavors, Costa's has a laid-back vibe with a menu of freshly baked pastries and light snacks priced between €3 and €8. Operating hours are from 8:00 AM to 8:00 PM, making it a convenient stop at any time. Their freshly brewed coffee pairs excellently with a flaky pastry for an afternoon break.

CHAPTER 9

9. PAPHOS AFTER DARK: NIGHTLIFE AND ENTERTAINMENT

BARS, LOUNGES, AND SUNSET SPOTS

Beachside Lounges and Bars

The beachside venues in Paphos provide the perfect mix of atmosphere and views. Sea View Lounge is a popular spot, located along the main harbor. This chic lounge allows guests to enjoy sunset cocktails while savoring fresh seafood. Open daily from 5:00 p.m. until midnight, it's an ideal venue to begin an evening out. Prices range from $10 for appetizers and up to $20 for specialty cocktails, with occasional happy hours on weekdays. Dress in comfortable beachwear for a relaxed, welcoming vibe.

Another favorite is Blue Wave Bar along the coast, near Coral Bay. This spot is known for its lively ambiance, and patrons enjoy the gentle evening sea breeze as the sun dips below the horizon. Blue Wave Bar stays open until 2:00

a.m., offering everything from traditional Cypriot drinks to international spirits, with prices starting at $8. This bar is also famous for its friendly staff and weekly live music, making it a fantastic place for a casual yet spirited evening.

Rooftop Views

To take in the city's skyline along with a brilliant sunset, head to Skyline Rooftop Bar, a modern rooftop venue located in the heart of Paphos. This location is well-known for its elegant design, unique cocktails, and excellent views. Open from 6:00 p.m. to 1:00 a.m., Skyline offers a sophisticated menu of Mediterranean-inspired drinks and dishes, with prices starting at $12. The rooftop vibe is perfect for couples and groups who want to experience a more refined setting. Reservations are recommended as it can fill up quickly, especially during weekends.

Sunset Deck is another rooftop destination, located on the edge of the Old Town. Known for its relaxed atmosphere, Sunset Deck offers unobstructed views of the horizon and the city's old-world architecture. The bar is open from 4:00 p.m. to midnight, with prices ranging from $9 for craft beers to $15 for specialty cocktails. It's a fantastic option for those looking for an intimate evening or a spot to enjoy the golden hour. Aim to arrive around 6:00 p.m. to get a good seat for sunset views.

Hidden Sunset Spots

For a quieter setting away from the main areas, Paphos has a few secret spots that locals favor. Aphrodite's Rock Viewpoint is a popular one, where you can take in the view of the famous rock formation as the sun sets over the sea. This spot doesn't require entry fees or specific hours, so it's a perfect choice for travelers who enjoy a more independent experience. Consider bringing a small picnic or grabbing a few drinks at a nearby cafe before arriving.

St. George's Sunset Terrace is another gem, offering both historic charm and a calm, beautiful view of the Mediterranean. The terrace is attached to a local taverna, where you can enjoy a meal with wine starting at $15. The terrace is generally open from noon until 11:00 p.m., but sunset views are best enjoyed between 6:00 p.m. and 8:00 p.m., depending on the season.

Nightlife Tips and Practical Information

While many venues in Paphos are welcoming to visitors, it's wise to dress appropriately depending on the setting. Beachside lounges are often relaxed, while rooftop bars may have a dress code favoring smart-casual attire. For budgeting, expect to spend between $10 and $30 per drink, especially for specialty cocktails or wines. Many bars also offer happy hours, typically between 5:00 p.m. and 7:00 p.m., which can be a great way to sample their menus at a more affordable rate.

WHERE TO FIND TRADITIONAL MUSIC AND DANCE

Attending local festivals, where exciting performances frequently take place, is one of the best ways to experience this musical culture. Paphos holds several events all year long that feature traditional Cypriot dance and music. Usually free to the public, these events give locals and tourists alike the chance to enjoy a variety of acts outside, frequently with picturesque views of the coast. Festivals like the Kataklysmos, or Festival of the Flood, offer a great chance to take in dancing and music that honor the island's unique culture. With an environment full of energetic and well-known Cypriot dances like the sousta and rhythmic folk tunes played on instruments like the violin and the laouto, a type of lute, these events urge communities to come together and rejoice.

The tavernas and smaller music venues dotted across Paphos offer yet another satisfying experience. Particularly in the warmer months, a lot of traditional tavernas have live music every week or even every night. Performers frequently infuse their music with emotional intensity in these small venues, delivering instrumentals and folk tunes that are influenced by the distinctive sounds and feelings of Cyprus.

You may get up close to the music and sense the energy between the performers and their audience at these usually casual concerts. You can witness or even participate in local dancers' performances on the dance floors of several tavernas. Because you can sense the island's pulse through its people, you can connect with the music and dance on a more personal level.

Cultural centers in Paphos occasionally host performances of traditional dance and music for people seeking a more regimented experience. The historical context and significance of each song and movement are frequently highlighted in these performances. The rich and vibrant costumes of the dancers offer visual context because each piece is intended to depict a different facet of Cypriot life, such as weddings, religious festivals, farming, and fishing. Visitors can easily arrange and take in a real taste of local artistry because performances at cultural facilities are typically planned at specified times.

Live performances can also be found at artisanal fairs and seasonal markets. These gatherings of singers, craftspeople, and artists frequently include brief but enthralling performances of traditional dance and music. These markets, which are typical during holidays and other festive times, offer a vibrant setting where stalls offering regional specialties and handcrafted crafts are paired with traditional music.

BEACH PARTIES, CLUBS, AND LATE-NIGHT FUN

Beach parties create a thrilling scene on the sand as the wave's crash against the coast under the moonlight. Well-known beach bars along the shore provide the ideal fusion of lively and laid-back moods. These events are particularly well-liked on Sundays, and you can anticipate live DJs, themed evenings, and even fire performances to add some flair.

Depending on the occasion, venues frequently charge a cover fee that ranges from €10 to €20. Some establishments even include a drink with entrance. These gatherings, which frequently begin at 8 PM and go into the morning, are perfect for a vibrant night or a wind-down in the evening.

If clubs are more your style, Paphos offers a wide range of venues with anything from house music to international hits. Mostly found in Kato Paphos and the main city area, these well-known locations feature international DJs, particularly in the summer. Depending on the artist lineup, entry fees might range from €10 to €15, with some special concerts costing €25 or more. After midnight, a lot of clubs begin to fill up, and it's not unusual for the activity to last until four in the morning or later. Choose venues that provide bottle service and VIP tables for a more upscale experience; they are perfect for big events.

Rooftop bars in Paphos provide a calm, picturesque option for those seeking a more leisurely experience, with views of the city lights or the sea.

Here, you may wind down after an evening of exploring or have a cocktail while admiring the calm surroundings before going out for a more exciting night. The ideal pre-party vibe is created by the fact that many of these locations open at 6 PM and remain open until midnight or later. Drinks range in price, with cocktails usually costing between €8 and €15. It's a fantastic choice for anyone who wishes to start their evening in a chic yet serene manner.

Consider going to a seasonal event or themed night if you're looking for a unique experience. A festive atmosphere is added to the evening by the numerous venues that offer special events for holidays or cultural festivals. Full-moon parties with neon lights, glow-in-the-dark décor, and thrilling performances are frequently held at outdoor clubs during the summer.

Midsummer celebrations and New Year's Eve are also lavishly celebrated, complete with fireworks, live acts, and long hours. Depending on the headliners and venue, ticket costs for these events might vary significantly, so it's a good idea to check ahead.

To make the most of your evening, think about organizing a few things ahead of time and asking your lodging for suggestions and guest lists that might provide free or reduced admission. In the evening, taxis and shuttle buses are easily accessible; however, during peak hours, expect to wait a little longer. Since many of these events require standing or dancing, it's best to dress comfortably.

CHAPTER 10

10. SHOPPING IN PAPHOS

LOCAL MARKETS: SOUVENIRS, SPICES, AND HANDCRAFTED TREASURES

Exploring local markets allows visitors to discover handcrafted objects that capture the character of Paphos and Cypriot craftsmanship. Handmade ceramics are among the most popular souvenirs, with elaborate designs that depict the island's history and creative traditions. Smaller ceramics are normally priced between €5 and €20, however larger, more complex ones might cost €30 or more, depending on the artistry involved. Sellers frequently like negotiating, so a nice talk can occasionally result in a good discount.

The spice booths provide a sensory treat. These spices, ranging from oregano and thyme to the peculiar aroma of halloumi seasoning, define Cypriot cuisine's indigenous characteristics. A small bag of dried herbs typically costs between €2 and €5, making it an affordable alternative for travelers wishing to bring home a flavor of the

Mediterranean. Vendors are frequently ready to explain how each spice is used in traditional dishes, making this a fun and educational trip to the market.

Visitors looking for one-of-a-kind products enjoy handmade jewelry as well. Local artists create a variety of goods, including beaded necklaces and elaborate metalwork influenced by ancient motifs. Prices vary, with smaller, simpler pieces ranging from €10 to €15, and more intricate things costing €25 to €50 or more. When choosing jewelry, search for sellers who are willing to give information about the materials used, as some may employ locally sourced stones or symbols with cultural significance.

Local markets also provide a variety of olive oil products, which are an important element of Cypriot life. Bottles of pure, locally produced olive oil are frequently available for €6–€12, depending on size. For a more opulent choice, consider blends infused with lemon, garlic, or herbs, which make excellent culinary gifts. Olive oil soaps and lotions are very popular, as they provide a more personal, scented memory of your visit.

Another treasure to hunt for is Cypriot lace, which is recognized for its exquisite patterns and traditional elegance. Tablecloths, napkins, and other linens have an astounding level of intricacy, with costs starting at about €10 for simple things and up to €50 or more for larger, more complex pieces. These make great keepsakes or considerate gifts, especially for individuals who value quality textile craftsmanship.

Before you go shopping, here are a few pointers to help you have a successful trip. Many local markets in Paphos operate mostly in the mornings, beginning about 8 a.m. and closing between 1 and 2 p.m., however, some may stay open a little later during peak seasons. Arriving early allows for a more relaxing visit and a wider opportunity to browse the goods without the afternoon throng. While most sellers accept cash, it is advisable to carry smaller notes to facilitate transactions. Some retailers may accept cards, but this is less usual, so plan accordingly.

Exploring the Boutiques: An Overview of Prices and Unique Pieces

The boutiques of Paphos are known for carrying exclusive clothing, accessories, and décor items. Prices vary widely depending on the designer and rarity of the pieces, but there's something to suit various budgets. You'll find locally-made jewelry starting around €20, while more luxurious designer garments and unique handcrafted items may range from €50 to over €200. This variety in pricing makes it possible for every shopper to bring home a taste of Paphos's style.

Explore stores tucked within quieter lanes. Here, independent artisans offer handmade jewelry, clothing, and accessories that highlight traditional designs with a modern twist. At the other end, luxury fashion boutiques and designer stores showcase high-end apparel, exquisite accessories, and beautiful home accents. Each piece reflects the elegance and warmth of Cypriot craftsmanship with a contemporary edge.

Tips for Finding Exceptional Pieces

1. Timing Your Visit – Shopping hours in Paphos often follow a traditional pattern, with most shops open from 9:00 a.m. to 7:00 p.m. Monday to Saturday. Some may close for a midday break between 1:00 p.m. and 3:00 p.m., especially in smaller neighborhoods. If you're looking for a more leisurely shopping experience, visiting in the afternoon offers a quieter atmosphere.

2. Weekday Mornings for Deals – Many stores refresh their inventory on weekends, so a weekday morning trip often uncovers the latest pieces. This is also a quieter time, allowing for a more relaxed shopping experience.

3. Getting Personal Style Advice – Many boutique owners are passionate about their collections and love to share the stories behind each item. Don't hesitate to ask about the origins of a piece or for styling tips; they're often thrilled to provide insights that add value to your purchase.

4. Be Prepared to Bargain – While designer boutiques generally have fixed prices, smaller stores and markets

may allow for bargaining. Friendly negotiation can be part of the shopping culture, especially for larger purchases or when buying multiple items. It's a great way to interact with the locals and perhaps discover a hidden treasure at a better price.

5. Seasonal Sales – Twice a year, in January and July, Paphos shops often hold sales where prices drop significantly. This is the best time to look for higher-end items at a fraction of the cost.

Spotlight on Must-Visit Boutiques

1. Olive Tree Gallery – This store offers a selection of handcrafted home décor, jewelry, and gifts inspired by traditional Cypriot art. Located near the historic heart of Paphos, the shop combines local artistry with modern design. Expect to find unique pottery, handwoven textiles, and more, with prices generally starting from €15. Hours are 10:00 a.m. to 6:00 p.m., Monday to Saturday.

2. Kivotos Art Gallery – Known for its eclectic mix of art, jewelry, and fashion, this gallery showcases pieces from

both local and international artists. Perfect for those looking for unique gifts or statement pieces, the gallery's prices range from €30 for small art pieces to €150 for larger items. The gallery is open daily from 10:00 a.m. to 7:00 p.m.

3. Kalypso Boutique – For high-end fashion with a Mediterranean touch, Kalypso Boutique offers designer wear, handmade jewelry, and accessories that exude elegance. Here, you'll find everything from dresses and handbags to carefully crafted jewelry pieces, with prices starting at around €40. The boutique is open from 9:00 a.m. to 7:00 p.m., closed on Sundays.

4. Cinnamon & Mint – This cozy shop carries a mix of vintage-inspired apparel, beachwear, and unique gifts, perfect for those looking for something a bit different. Prices here are affordable, with items ranging from €20 to €100. Open from 11:00 a.m. to 5:00 p.m., this boutique is a favorite among locals and travelers alike.

5. Limelight – A chic clothing store that emphasizes contemporary style, Limelight offers stylish apparel and accessories, blending Cypriot traditions with modern influences. With prices starting at €30, it's easy to find a beautiful piece to remember your trip. Opening hours are 10:00 a.m. to 6:30 p.m., closed on Sundays.

CYPRIOT WINE, OLIVE OIL, AND SWEETS TO BRING HOME

Cypriot Wine

The vineyards of Cyprus, with their ancient history of winemaking, yield a variety of exceptional wines that are crafted with care and traditional methods. One of the standout varieties is Commandaria, a dessert wine known for its deep, honeyed flavor.

Often referred to as the oldest wine still in production, Commandaria has a sweet profile, perfect for sipping after dinner or pairing with rich desserts. Many visitors also enjoy trying the island's local reds and whites, often made from unique grape varieties such as Xynisteri and Mavro.

Sampling these wines at a local vineyard offers a firsthand experience of their unique flavors, which are shaped by Cyprus's warm, sunny climate and mineral-rich soils. To bring a bottle back home is to bring a piece of Cypriot heritage and share it with loved ones.

Pure Olive Oil

Another gift that truly reflects the essence of Cyprus is olive oil. The Mediterranean region is famous for its high-quality oils, and Cyprus is no exception. The island's olive trees, some of which are hundreds of years old, produce oils that are both fragrant and flavorful. Locally sourced and often made by small producers, the oils are typically cold-pressed, preserving the rich and grassy taste that makes Cypriot olive oil special.

Many bottles are beautifully packaged, making them ideal gifts for family and friends or as a reminder of the island's landscapes and culinary traditions. Olive oil from Cyprus not only enhances cooking with its robust flavor but also connects you to the island's agricultural roots and centuries-old traditions.

Sweet Treats

Cypriot sweets bring an entirely different kind of delight. One favorite is loukoumi, a soft, chewy treat often known as "Cyprus Delight." Made with sugar, and cornstarch, and infused with flavors like rose or citrus, this delicacy has a melt-in-the-mouth quality that's light and aromatic. Many shops in Paphos offer gift boxes of loukoumi, making it a colorful and tasty gift.

Another classic sweet is soutzoukos, which is made from grape must, nuts, and a bit of patience, as each piece is repeatedly dipped to create its layered texture. This treat carries a touch of natural sweetness from the grapes, balanced with the earthy taste of nuts, and is a great addition to a cheese platter or enjoyed on its own. Cyprus is also known for pastelli, a brittle snack made from sesame seeds and carob syrup. This sweet is loved for its chewy texture and nutty flavor, which captures the island's sunny disposition and agricultural abundance.

CHAPTER 11

Local Laws and Respect for Customs

Paphos has a friendly and welcoming culture, and observing local customs helps to foster beneficial interactions. Public shows of affection, for example, are typically acceptable, but excessive gestures can draw attention. When visiting holy locations, dress modestly; cover your shoulders and avoid wearing shorts. Smoking is not permitted in indoor public spaces, therefore look for designated smoking spots.

Alcohol usage is generally liberal in Cyprus, but drinking in public places other than approved bars and restaurants is discouraged. If you're driving, be aware of the legal blood alcohol level, which is lower than in other countries. Penalties for disobeying traffic and safety rules are vigorously enforced, so adhering to local driving restrictions is critical for a trouble-free journey.

Traffic Regulations and Road Safety

Cyprus has left-hand traffic regulations. While it may take some time to adjust if you're used to driving on the right, the roads are well-marked and there is English signage. Seatbelts are required for all passengers, and using a cell phone while driving is illegal unless you have a hands-free device. Speed limits differ depending on whether you're in an urban, rural, or highway environment, so pay attention to signs.

Pedestrians should use marked crossings, as automobiles have the right of way on most roads, particularly those outside of major cities. Walking paths and sidewalks are normally safe, but exercise caution on narrow or steep roads, especially in villages and seaside areas.

Health and Personal Safety Tips:

The Mediterranean sun in Paphos may be intense, especially during the summer. Wearing sunscreen, hats, and sunglasses will help you avoid sunburn. Carrying a reusable water bottle to stay hydrated is also a good idea, as the heat may be extreme, especially if you're visiting outdoor attractions.

Paphos has well-equipped pharmacies and hospitals. Pharmacies are easily identified by the green cross emblem, and many employees understand English. For help, dial 199 or 112 to reach emergency services. Travel insurance is widely recommended because it can cover medical expenditures and provide peace of mind in the face of unanticipated circumstances.

Keeping valuables safe and avoiding scams.

Paphos is typically safe, but like with any tourist site, you should exercise caution with your things. Keep valuables in your hotel safe when not in use, and avoid carrying large amounts of cash. Pickpocketing is uncommon, but it can happen in crowded settings, so keep an eye out in high-traffic areas.

When arranging trips or activities, it's best to choose reputable companies. While locals provide many fantastic experiences, make sure that any tour or rental company you choose has a good reputation. Some travelers encounter unofficial guides or unlawful services, so reading reviews or reserving through reputable suppliers will help you avoid problems.

Emergency Contacts and Relevant Resources

Keeping a list of significant contacts can be extremely useful. The tourist police in Paphos are there to help visitors, and many speak English. They can advise on local legislation, safety precautions, and other travel-related matters. Contact information for your country's embassy or consulate, as well as any pertinent travel hotlines, should be kept handy.

Those traveling into the countryside or hiking along Paphos' magnificent paths should notify someone of their plans, especially if they are exploring alone. Cell service is available in most areas, but it might be patchy in isolated locations. Planning your itinerary ahead of time will ensure a safe and pleasurable outdoor experience.

EMERGENCY CONTACTS AND HEALTH FACILITIES

Emergency Contacts:

In Paphos, various emergency services are available to help travelers in need. The main emergency number to call in Cyprus is 112, which links to police, fire, and ambulance services. This number works nationally and is free to dial from any phone, ensuring immediate aid in severe situations. Additionally, 199 is the precise number to call the police in Paphos if necessary.

The Cyprus Tourism Organization (CTO) Information Office can answer non-urgent medical issues or address minor health concerns. They are knowledgeable about local options and can refer you to relevant services based on your needs. Many hotels and motels in Paphos also have a list of reliable connections, ranging from private doctors to 24-hour pharmacies, offering you another choice for assistance if you're staying nearby.

Health Facilities in Paphos

Paphos offers a number of medical facilities, including governmental hospitals and private clinics that provide a wide range of health services. Paphos General Hospital is the principal public hospital, offering emergency services, specialized care, and a variety of medical specialties.

This hospital, located near the town center, is a reliable resource for both residents and visitors, especially for emergencies or more serious health concerns. Public hospitals may have lower prices than private institutions, especially if you have European Health Insurance (EHIC) or comparable coverage.

Private clinics in Paphos are also accessible, offering speedier service and more possibilities for specialized treatment. The Blue Cross Medical Center and Iasis Hospital are two reputable private hospitals. They provide a variety of treatments, including diagnostic imaging, minor surgery, and urgent care. These private institutions are known for their high standards and multilingual staff, making them an excellent alternative when rapid, attentive care is required.

Pharmacy and Medical Supplies

Pharmacies are freely accessible throughout Paphos, with many staying open late or even 24 hours, particularly in tourist districts. In Cyprus, several over-the-counter pharmaceuticals, such as pain relievers, basic antibiotics, and first-aid supplies, are available without a prescription. Pharmacists in Paphos are skilled and frequently speak English, making it easy to explain any requirements.

If you need a pharmacy after hours, check for businesses with a "Pharmacy" sign. Each region in Paphos has at least one pharmacy open at night on a rotating basis, which may be found via the local pharmacy network or tourist information centers.

Tips for Staying Safe

As with any destination, it is advisable to have a small medical kit with essentials such as sticky bandages, antiseptic wipes, and any prescription prescriptions. It's also a good idea to find out where the nearest hospital or clinic is in relation to your accommodation. Knowing these important data will help you deal with any unexpected health issues and make the most of your time in Paphos.

INTERNET, SIM CARDS, AND STAYING CONNECTED

Buying a prepaid SIM card can be a useful option. SIM cards are readily available at the airport, large businesses, and convenience stores, so obtaining one upon arrival is simple. Popular providers such as CYTA, Epic, and PrimeTel provide a variety of plans based on data limit, length, and price, allowing you to select the best solution for your needs. The majority of these plans contain enough data for social networking, navigation, and browsing, making it easy to stay connected throughout your travel.

Visitors' short-term plans are typically good for 7, 15, or 30 days, with the opportunity to recharge if additional data is required or to extend your stay. Registration for a SIM card is simple and only requires your passport or a form of ID; activation is usually immediate.

If you don't want to swap SIMs, Wi-Fi is generally available in Paphos. Customers frequently have free access at hotels, cafes, and restaurants, and speeds are usually enough for streaming, video chats, and web browsing. Some public spaces and tourist destinations may also provide free Wi-Fi, but coverage varies based on location. To stay up to date, ask the staff at your hotel or neighborhood café about Wi-Fi availability. Some carriers now offer temporary mobile hotspots that may be rented for the duration of your journey, which is especially beneficial for frequent travelers or those visiting rural regions.

Travelers frequently use apps such as WhatsApp, Skype, and Viber to make calls home without incurring the hefty expenses associated with international phone plans. These platforms work seamlessly over Wi-Fi, and because Cyprus is a member of the EU, tourists from Europe can frequently use their home plans under EU roaming arrangements, which typically allow for domestic prices throughout member nations.

CHAPTER 12

12. DAY TRIPS AND EXCURSIONS BEYOND PAPHOS

LIMASSOL: CYPRUS' COSMOPOLITAN COASTAL HUB

Take a leisurely walk down the coastal promenade in Limassol to start. With a vibrant array of cafés, shops, and gardens on one side and vistas of the Mediterranean on the other, the paved path runs the length of the shore. It's a laid-back yet vibrant environment that's ideal for enjoying the views of the ocean and experiencing the vibrant coastal vibe of the city. The promenade is a great place to see Limassol's daily life because it is well-liked by both locals and tourists.

The history of Limassol is intriguing for those who are interested in it. Limassol Castle, located in the center of the old town, silently records centuries of transformation, from medieval wars to peaceful cohabitation. The Cyprus Medieval Museum, housed in the castle, provides visitors with an insight into the island's history with displays of antiquities, antiquated coins, and armor sets. In addition to its historical significance, the castle and its environs offer insight into the architectural trends that have shaped Cyprus over time.

Another must-see location nearby is the ancient market district. The best of Cypriot workmanship and food can be found in this vibrant district, which is filled with the scents of fresh vegetables, local spices, and handcrafted handicrafts. Visitors can purchase a distinctive memento or try regional delicacies while perusing the stalls. The market is still a vibrant aspect of the city's culture, and it's simple to see how these classic features mesh well with Limassol's modern atmosphere.

Head to Limassol Marina, a posh neighborhood renowned for its upscale stores, sophisticated waterfront eateries, and magnificent yachts. The marina's distinctive ambiance, which symbolizes Limassol's forward-thinking nature, is created by the contrast between the modern buildings and the serene water. It's an excellent spot to relax, eat, or just enjoy the lovely surroundings.

Wine lovers will discover that Limassol serves as the entry point to the island's renowned wine area. The city core is only a short drive away from a group of hillside towns renowned for its winemaking heritage and vineyards. Visitors can tour vineyards, taste Cypriot wines, and discover the island's longstanding connection to viticulture in locations like Omodos and Koilani. In addition to offering a gentler pace, these communities have cobblestone walkways and friendly residents who are happy to share their wine customs.

Those who enjoy art and culture can visit the Limassol Cultural Center, which frequently organizes events, performances, and exhibitions that highlight both domestic and foreign artists. Cyprus's vibrant arts scene and commitment to conserving and advancing cultural forms are embodied by this facility.

KYKKOS MONASTERY AND THE MOUNTAINS

A day's journey from Paphos to the Kykkos Monastery and the neighboring mountains provides a unique blend of natural beauty and rich cultural legacy, resulting in adventure and awe. The journey into Cyprus's heartland starts with a lovely drive through winding roads and beautiful mountain communities. As the environment changes from coastal vistas to thick pine forests, each turn offers a different aspect of Cyprus, far from the vibrant beaches of Paphos.

Kykkos Monastery, located high on the slopes of the Troodos Mountains, is one of the island's most revered religious destinations, attracting visitors from all over the world. Byzantine Emperor Alexios I Komnenos founded the monastery in the 11th century, and it stands as a tribute to centuries of dedication and architectural magnificence. Its greatest feature is the renowned icon of the Virgin Mary, which is supposed to have been painted by the Apostle Luke. This precious artifact, richly ornamented and hidden from direct view, symbolizes the people's strong spiritual connection to this location.

Visitors are greeted by the monastery's massive stone walls, vibrant murals, and glittering gilded iconostasis in the main chapel. The monastery's interiors are decorated with elaborate paintings that tell the stories of saints and religious icons, allowing visitors to connect with Cyprus' rich Orthodox Christian past. Taking in these intricacies provides a look into the artistry and craftsmanship that have been preserved over hundreds of years.

The surrounding mountain pathways and viewpoints make this journey unforgettable. Walking through the cool, pine-scented air and listening to nature's sounds provides a tranquil contrast to the bustling metropolis of Paphos. Travelers can explore the paths surrounding the monastery, which provide panoramic views of the island's steep topography and forested slopes. The Troodos Mountains also have hidden pathways and isolated picnic areas where you can relax and take in the breathtaking scenery.

Aside from its religious and natural attractiveness, the area surrounding Kykkos Monastery is rich in local culture. Nearby communities are renowned for their traditional crafts, homemade sweets, and Cypriot hospitality. Some tours stop in these alpine communities, allowing you to sample local cuisine or purchase a handcrafted item. Sampling real Cypriot delicacies, from sweet loukoumi to savory cheeses and wines, adds a touch of local culture to the experience.

The ride back to Paphos provides one more opportunity to enjoy the tranquil beauty of the mountains and valleys, with vistas that will stay with you long after the day is over. A journey to Kykkos Monastery and the Troodos Mountains reveals a distinct side of Cyprus, one steeped in spirituality and natural beauty.

NICOSIA: A CITY DIVIDED

A trip from Paphos to Nicosia provides insight into the complicated history, evolving culture, and distinct atmosphere of Cyprus's capital. Nicosia, located a few hours from the shore, is the world's last divided capital, separated between the Republic of Cyprus and Northern Cyprus by the "Green Line." This line, marked by checkpoints and visible obstacles, is a distinctive feature of the city's landscape, providing tourists with a view into its complex modern history.

Exploring Nicosia is like entering a cultural crossroads, where you can see layers of history mirrored in both the old and new parts of the city. Begin your tour by walking through the Venetian Walls, a 16th-century fortress that surrounds the old city. These walls lead to the city center, which is lined with meandering streets, little cafés, and one-of-a-kind stores.

You may meander around Ledra Street, a bustling neighborhood studded with shops, restaurants, and historical sites that all provide a glimpse into Nicosia's blend of history and progress.

Crossing the Green Line checkpoint on Ledra Street reveals Nicosia's split nature. Travelers with a valid passport can explore both sides, which have distinct customs and characteristics. On the southern side, institutions such as the Cyprus Museum display historical relics, offering light on Cyprus's extensive history. The museum's displays span thousands of years, revealing the rich history of this area.

On the northern side of the city, you'll find attractions such as Buyuk Han, a 16th-century caravanserai that has been rebuilt and now houses modest stores, galleries, and cafés. Its design reflects the Ottoman influence that formed much of Nicosia's history, and the bustling ambiance allows visitors to unwind while experiencing Cypriot hospitality. For those interested in religious history, the Selimiye Mosque, previously the Cathedral of Saint Sophia, is a stunning blend of Gothic and Ottoman construction. This mosque offers a unique perspective on how cultures and faiths have interacted throughout the years.

As the capital, Nicosia has a strong arts scene. Art galleries and local workshops display modern Cypriot innovation, featuring pieces that reflect both contemporary and historical topics. A visit to these galleries provides an opportunity to engage with contemporary manifestations of Nicosia's past and evolving socioeconomic context.

AYIA NAPA AND THE EAST COAST BEACHES

Discovering Ayia Napa and the East Coast Beaches from Paphos is an unforgettable adventure for those looking to experience more of Cyprus than its western shores. These day travels along the eastern coast provide sandy beaches, unique cultural attractions, and exciting activities. Travelers who drive throughout the island will discover a colorful contrast to Paphos, with fresh sites that provide their vitality and charm.

Beginning with Ayia Napa, this seaside town is noted for its dazzling beaches, vibrant environment, and reputation as one of Cyprus' most active hubs. Ayia Napa, formerly a little fishing village, has evolved into a popular destination for visitors looking for a blend of coastal relaxation and exciting activities. Nissi Beach, with its beautiful seas and fine sands, is a popular tourist destination and ideal for swimming, sunbathing, or simply taking a refreshing plunge in the Mediterranean. Makronissos Beach, which is close by, offers a tranquil setting with golden sands and is popular with families. For those interested in learning more about local culture, Ayia Napa Monastery, which dates back to the 16th century, provides a calm getaway from the seaside buzz, tucked in the heart of town and featuring gorgeous architecture and a peaceful garden.

The Cape Greco National Forest Park, located near Ayia Napa, is a natural gem along the eastern coast. Cape Greco, known for its gorgeous hiking trails and pristine waters, appeals to both nature enthusiasts and adventurers. The coastal cliffs and sea caves are fascinating to explore, and visitors frequently take time to swim, snorkel, or photograph the unusual rock formations. The famous

"Blue Lagoon" in Cape Greco is recognized for its crystal-clear waters and is a great place for a brief dip or a boat cruise, with breathtaking views of the coastline.

Protaras, located further along the eastern coast, is also a popular destination, particularly for Fig Tree Bay. Its clean, shallow waters and relaxing atmosphere make it a popular location for families and beachgoers. This harbor provides excellent snorkeling conditions, with gentle waves and diverse marine life. Protaras is also recognized for its picturesque beach promenades, local cafés, and friendly stores, making it an excellent place to have a leisurely lunch or browse Cypriot souvenirs and crafts.

With easy access to a range of beaches, gorgeous parks, and cultural attractions, a day excursion from Paphos to Ayia Napa and the east coast provides a perfect mixture of rest and activity. These trips highlight Cyprus's diversity, from vibrant town centers to natural beauties along the Mediterranean coast, providing visitors with a comprehensive understanding of the island's distinct character.

CHAPTER 13

13. RESPONSIBLE AND SUSTAINABLE TRAVEL IN PAPHOS

SUPPORTING LOCAL BUSINESSES AND ARTISANS

Family-owned stores and studios line Paphos' streets and marketplaces, selling a diverse range of handmade goods, unusual clothes, and regional specialties. Many of these firms are deeply rooted in tradition, with abilities passed down through generations. Artisans frequently make their products by hand, using locally sourced materials and ancient processes to give them a one-of-a-kind appearance. Travelers may come across elaborate lacework, hand-painted pottery, or stunning silver jewelry, all of which represent the island's heritage in concrete ways.

Guests can learn directly from the craftspeople themselves. Many workshops in Paphos invite visitors to observe their creative processes firsthand, and some even provide short lectures or demos. Watching a competent potter mold clay or a jeweler delicately create a piece of silver jewelry reveals the work, patience, and ingenuity required. It's an opportunity to engage with the creators and develop a greater appreciation for their work.

Local food companies also contribute greatly to the area's charm, providing visitors with a taste of traditional Cypriot cuisine. These modest businesses, ranging from olive oil and honey makers to bakers specializing in traditional pastries, celebrate the island's gastronomic heritage. Sampling homemade items straight from the source not only reveals distinct flavors but also promotes sustainable eating practices. Many of these enterprises use locally farmed ingredients, providing a fresher, more flavorful experience than mass-produced products. Every meal becomes more meaningful for travelers when they know their purchases benefit local farmers and food artisans.

These tiny businesses and artists are centralized in Paphos markets. Whether at a weekend farmer's market or a bustling bazaar, visitors can connect with the creators while browsing a wide range of products. The environment at these markets is friendly and engaging, with sellers willing to tell their stories, answer questions, and provide product suggestions. Purchasing directly from craftsmen offers fair compensation and develops personal connections that giant stores or online shops cannot replicate.

ECO-FRIENDLY TOURS AND ACTIVITIES

Paphos serves as a gateway to some of Cyprus' most stunning landscapes, such as the craggy coasts and forested hillsides. Hiking routes on the Akamas Peninsula provide an opportunity to explore the region's distinctive wildlife. Guided eco-tours take visitors along routes rich in natural flora and fauna, highlighting Cyprus' plant species and allowing opportunities to see varied birdlife. These tours frequently adhere to low-impact tourism standards, ensuring minimal damage to wildlife while also contributing to the preservation of natural areas. Knowledgeable local guides give insights into the region's environment, making each hike interesting and meaningful.

Water-based activities are also provided, with a focus on minimizing environmental impact. Eco-friendly snorkeling and diving tours are available in and around Paphos to get a closer look at the underwater environment. These operators prioritize marine conservation and adhere to tight rules to safeguard coral reefs and marine habitats. Small-group sizes and eco-certified equipment are common, allowing tourists to enjoy the blue seas while also protecting precious marine life.

Some expeditions also include briefings on the importance of protecting Cyprus' coastal ecosystems, encouraging a more responsible attitude to marine research.

Exploring the region's vineyards and farms reveals visitors to Paphos' agricultural side, where local farmers use sustainable farming techniques. Many vineyards employ organic growing and lower their carbon footprint through methods such as natural pest control and water conservation. A vineyard tour frequently includes tasting local wines and learning about the island's viticulture traditions, all while promoting environmentally sustainable production. In addition, certain farms in the Paphos area encourage visitors to learn about traditional farming practices and local produce, including olives, grapes, herbs, and honey. These trips provide an opportunity to engage with Cypriot culture while also supporting small-scale, sustainable manufacturers.

Cycling lovers will discover that Paphos is a bike-friendly city with various routes intended for safe, picturesque cycling. Renting a bicycle is an environmentally sensible way to move around, decreasing dependency on motorized cars while also allowing riders to see more of the countryside.

Many bike lanes go to more tranquil locations and provide panoramic views of the sea or adjacent hills. Guided bicycle tours are provided, with expert instructors who may provide information on the surrounding environment and cultural landmarks along the way. Bikes are frequently outfitted with all necessary equipment, and routes are designed to minimize environmental effects, ensuring a fun yet responsible adventure.

Eco-conscious guests will enjoy and appreciate the several green-friendly lodgings in Paphos. Many hotels and resorts have shifted to renewable energy, decreased single-use plastics, and installed water-saving technologies. Staying at an eco-friendly hotel not only promotes sustainable travel but often improves the experience with natural surroundings and locally produced facilities. Several lodgings collaborate on conservation programs, allowing guests to learn more about ongoing efforts to preserve Paphos' natural beauty.

TIPS FOR REDUCING YOUR CARBON FOOTPRINT WHILE TRAVELING

By giving priority to environmentally friendly modes of transportation, you may reduce your impact on the environment in one of the simplest ways possible. Because buses are a more economical mode of transportation than renting a car, you might want to think about using Paphos's public transportation choices rather than hiring a car.

You can also explore the area at a leisurely pace while avoiding emissions totally by walking or riding a bike, both of which are fantastic options. If you require a vehicle, you should consider renting a hybrid or electric vehicle, as these types of vehicles are becoming more accessible and produce fewer emissions of pollutants.

When it comes to lodging, choosing accommodations that are sensitive to the environment can go a long way toward accomplishing this goal. Paphos is home to a large number of hotels and guesthouses that are implementing environmentally friendly policies and procedures, including water conservation systems, trash reduction initiatives, and energy-efficient lighting. Through the selection of lodgings that emphasize sustainability, you can show your support for businesses that share your dedication to protecting the environment. In addition, you should think about staying at family-owned guesthouses, which typically operate on a smaller scale and have a lesser carbon impact than huge hotels that are part of a chain.

It is also possible to reduce one's carbon footprint by adopting more environmentally responsible dining practices. Paphos features a range of local cafes selling fresh, seasonal produce that represents the island's characteristics while limiting food miles.

By dining at restaurants that get their ingredients locally, you support the regional economy and reduce the environmental cost of transporting things from abroad. Opting for plant-based meals where possible will further minimize your carbon footprint, as plant-based diets tend to use less energy and water in production.

Mindful waste management is key for sustainable travel. Paphos offers recycling facilities, so be sure to dispose of your garbage correctly, separating recyclables wherever possible. Avoid single-use plastics by bringing a reusable water bottle, as tap water in Paphos is generally safe to drink. Bringing reusable shopping bags can help lessen the need for plastic bags, which often wind up as garbage on beaches or in the water.

Respecting natural landscapes and wildlife in Paphos is another key part of eco-friendly travel. When visiting nature reserves, archaeological sites, or beaches, always stick to specified routes to avoid hurting indigenous flora and animals. Collecting shells or moving rocks might appear innocent but can undermine delicate ecosystems. Instead, snap photos and leave nothing but footprints, ensuring these natural beauties remain intact for future visitors.

CONCLUSION

As we pull the curtains on our research of Paphos, we hope that the vivid descriptions and precise insights given in this guide have fueled your wanderlust. From the sun-drenched sands of Coral Bay to the ancient echoes of the Tombs of the Kings, Paphos is not just a destination but a doorway to an experience steeped in history and filled with natural beauty.

We've journeyed together through scenic alleys, dined in tiny tavernas where the aroma of local delicacies fills the air, and stepped back in time within the walls of storied castles and ruins that whisper tales of old. The crystal-clear rivers and rocky terrain have encouraged us to join in excursions that promise to improve our spirits and restore our bodies.

Paphos is a country where legends meet luxury, and nature's beauty is mirrored by the friendliness of its people. Whether it's reveling in the relaxation of a coastal resort or hiking across the gorgeous Akamas Peninsula, there is something in Paphos for every visitor, every family, and every dreamer.

As you close this guide, remember that Paphos isn't simply a place you visit; it's an experience you live. So, pack your luggage, purchase your tickets, and set forth on a voyage that promises to be unforgettable. Let the charm of Paphos call you to its magical embrace, and may your adventures be as enriching and transforming as the stories you will tell for years to come.